MAKER CAMP

HERITAGE CRAFTS AND SKILL-BUILDING PROJECTS FOR *Kids*

DELANIE HOLTON-FESSLER

Roost Books
An imprint of Shambhala
Publications, Inc.
4720 Walnut Street
Boulder, Colorado 80301
roostbooks.com

Cover art: Delanie Holton
Book and cover design:
Ian Dingman

9 8 7 6 5 4 3 2 1

First Edition
Printed in China

∞ This edition is printed on
acid-free paper that meets the
American National Standards
Institute Z39.48 Standard.
♻ Roost Books makes
every effort to print on
recycled paper. For more
information please visit
www.shambhala.com.
Roost Books is distributed
worldwide by Penguin
Random House, Inc., and its
subsidiaries.

Library of Congress
Cataloging-in-Publication Data
Names: Holton-Fessler,
Delanie, author.
Title: Maker Camp: heritage
crafts and skill-building projects
for kids /
    Delanie Holton-Fessler.
Description: First edition. |
Boulder, Colorado: Roost
Books, [2021]
Identifiers: LCCN 2019057036
| ISBN 9781611807844
(hardcover: paper over board)
Subjects: LCSH: Handicraft—
Juvenile literature.
Classification: LCC TT171 .H55
200321 | DDC 745.5—dc23
LC record available at https://
lccn.loc.gov/2019057036

CONTENTS

PART ONE
HERITAGE SKILLS
34

PART TWO
FIBER ARTS
64

PART THREE

WOOD-WORKING

96

PART FOUR

TINKER, BUILD, AND PLAY

126

PREFACE

Education is radically about love.
—Paulo Freire

There are two things that mean the most to me: people and putting my hands to work. I couldn't imagine life without connection to others nor a life without making. I was the child who was always drawing, always putting something together; and in my youth I loved playing in the woods and being in nature. I believe that my art teachers and an out-of-school arts program in Boulder kept me afloat as a teenager struggling with big life stuff. As a young adult, I went to art school, managed the sculpture studio, studied education, and actively participated in the creative world here in Denver. I then continued working as an artist and started my career as an art teacher in high-poverty schools. In that time, I found that being a trustworthy caregiver was at the core of all of the work I do with kids. A person has to feel safe and loved before they can tap their creative brain. Knowing that all of my work is relationship-driven, I then spent the last five years running my community-based workshop, The Craftsman & Apprentice, as a testing ground for everything that I believed to be true about working with kids.

Working with children and being a mother have been my life's greatest work. I feel immensely grateful that I've been able to engage with thousands of kids from many different backgrounds and abilities.

There's nothing like bearing witness to a child in flow. The hard parts of life melt away, and there we are, in the moment, creating something new. It doesn't get much better than that.

I also believe that kids and adults deserve to work and live in beautiful and functional spaces and that they deserve to have ample time to make, play, and learn. I believe deeply in relationship-driven learning, and now I get to share all of my favorite projects, philosophy, and more with you. I challenge you as you read this book, as caregivers of the amazing things called children, to reflect on your own childhood. What are the moments that positively defined you? Who were those people who made you feel whole and trusted? How can you set the stage for the little people in your life to have those moments of definition and trust?

Our ideas, behaviors, and passions change over time. My thoughts about art education have changed profoundly over the years. What I now know is that in addition to traditional fine arts education, there's a world that many children are missing. You may still be old enough to remember home economics and shop class, where we learned practical skills and how to work safely and create items of use. We learned how to take care of our homes and one another. How are we teaching our children these skills? Through the seemingly antiquated notion of arts and crafts, we practice at life, we make life more beautiful, and we connect to one another. Let's get our hands dirty, make mistakes, and bring back some good old-fashioned making and doing.

MAKER
CAMP

INTRODUCTION

Why do we create? This is a big question, but one with a simple answer. We're human. Our innate ability to create and innovate is what makes us uniquely human. From a very early age, children build. Give a stack of blocks to a one-year-old and they will stack and sort. This simple process is a foundational example of how our brains are hardwired to create. Play is the earliest form of creativity. Children take familiar objects and use them in new and innovative ways. This process allows children to decode their world, to discover through play the way things work and how simple objects and materials can be combined to produce new and novel expressions.

I often hear from adults, "I'm just not creative." Somewhere along the line, many adults failed at making something, they failed to have access to creative outlets, they failed to be told that it's okay to make things that aren't perfect. Maybe the concept of creativity as it pertains to the creation of objects wasn't valued in their home or community. If you're one of those adults, it's not too late. It's not too late to build your creative skills, to empower yourself to create objects. I find no better way to reinforce my maker self than to make things with kids. Kids have an amazing ability to act without the self-conscious mind

telling them that what they're doing isn't good enough. Kids have the innate ability to work in process, to disregard the outcome in favor of the experience of creation. We as adults, as concrete thinkers, can take a cue from the playful nature of children to reengage the innate playful curiosity that we're all born with. And bonus, kids aren't harsh critics. They love what you do. They love that you're just trying.

What I love most about making things with children is that I am reminded each day that we're all learning. Being creative isn't an endgame but rather a way of being. It's messy, it's full of failure and success, and if given the right circumstances and frame of mind, it's so much fun.

The aim of this book is to help all children build skills that will enable them to be confident creators no matter where life takes them as adults. Not everyone is going to be a painter, a weaver, or a woodworker, but we're all tasked with problems to solve. I firmly believe that when we teach children to work with their hands, to tinker, and to play, we teach them to trust themselves, to trust their own intuition, and to solve problems—just as humans have always done. We humans are meant to be makers.

From fire building to advanced technology, humans have always had an innate desire to create, for the sake of advancement but also for the sake of self-expression and cultural identity. We create based on the world around us, with what we have available. Give a group of children a set of blocks, a cardboard box, or a set of paints, and each child will approach the materials in their unique way. This is an expression of personality, culture, skills, and behaviors modeled by adults and peers. Creative practices are containers for personal growth. Through creative practices, children learn about themselves, they express emotion, and they learn to question and to find ways to answer their questions independently.

The drive to play is the drive to create and connect. Through creative practices we connect to one another, to our elders, to our culture. Creativity doesn't happen in a vacuum. Creativity is by necessity built on the creativity of others. An integral aspect of creating with children is the social bonds that are created in the process. Children learn to share, to ask for help, to trust themselves to solve problems as they

arise. As caregivers and cocreators, we can help children develop these skills and behaviors through our own working practices, as well as by creating space and offering materials and practices that enable the creative process.

In this book I will guide you through a variety of projects and working practices that will enable you as a cocreator to encourage and celebrate creative and practical play with your children. Creativity is at the core of the practices in this book. What is creativity? It's simply posing the question, "What else is possible?"

In these pages we will explore historical craft and workshop traditions that are rooted in best practices when making with kids. Based on my eighteen-year career working with kids and families, this book encompasses the aesthetics, working practices, and projects I've come to love. The projects and essays in this book weave a story of human innovation and creativity from the very beginnings of building shelters in the woods to tinkering with recycled materials. Each project includes adaptations for varying ages and abilities, a lesson narrative, guiding questions, and suggested practices that allow you as a caregiver to deepen project inquiry. Find what speaks to you. Use this book as a resource to revisit again and again for the practices as much as for the projects.

12 BEST PRACTICES

FOR CREATIVE WORK:
The Shop Model

The founding principles to our work at The Craftsman & Apprentice are what we call "the Shop Model." When we first began to think about opening The Craftsman & Apprentice, my husband and I would talk at length about what we love about being makers. Jon is a master stonemason who learned his trade over the course of many years as an apprentice. We would ask ourselves, "How do we know what we know?" and "How do we do our best work?" We also talked about all the things we've loved about being part of a creative community. When we boiled it all down, we realized that making things and learning how to make things with our hands is best done in community, in real-life proximity to other people all learning and creating together while we change and grow over time. We're meant to seek feedback, to collaborate, to learn from our elders. When we learn from one another, we all benefit. It's human nature to build upon the practices and innovations of others.

The Shop Model, then, is a set of working practices developed out of working in studio and workshop spaces as an artist and educator, as well as from my own research on the history of handcraft. There are twelve working practices of the Shop Model. These practices aren't meant to be exhaustive or concrete. The importance or weight of each practice will vary depending on your child, their age, and your project or practice goals. These twelve practices are meant to serve as reminders of ways in which we can best collaborate and work as makers.

The Shop Model sets the stage for young makers to develop working habits that will serve them for a lifetime. Use the Shop Model as a guide, as a tool to reflect on the working practices of the children in your care.

1.

MAKE A PLAN: IT CAN AND WILL CHANGE

I'm a planner by nature. I need to know what's going to happen next. I'm never without a sticky note and a checklist. However, I've also learned to lean into the process. Best-laid plans can and do change. Having a plan helps guide our work; it gives us a road map. However, we must know that change and divergence from even the best-laid plans are all part of the process.

As a teacher, I have a special place in my heart for backward planning. This is a process in which you lay out the goal first, and backward engineer a plan to get you there. My mother-in-law would always say, "An inch is a cinch." Backward planning allows us to create a manageable plan of attack. Break your big goals into small actionable items. For instance, we've been working on a collaborative mini grocery shop for some while. Our team of shop kids made a lofty plan with all the bells and whistles of a real grocery shop. We then met to figure out where to begin and delegated the roles to individuals and groups. Some kids would be working on displays, some on canned goods, some on salt dough food sculptures. We then met with each team to develop a work plan for each component. Work plans are an easy way for kids to track their progress. Bring on the sticky notes! Kids, like most adults, can really only focus on two or three steps at a time. Grab a sticky note and have your kiddo draw or write out three steps at a

time to keep the momentum and focus going. This planning strategy is also super helpful for kids with organizational and focus needs.

Planning strategies can range from large-scale strategic and backward planning to a simple conversation about goals to following step-by-step instructions. Be as guided or as loose as your work requires. When using the plans in this book, be flexible. If something doesn't work for you or your kiddo, change it. Be flexible in your process and outcomes.

2.

DON'T BE AFRAID TO COLLABORATE

We live in a world that is all too often an individualistic one. We're taught to protect our thoughts and ideas. Collaboration is a core part of the Shop Model for good reason. People are not meant to work in a vacuum. Collaboration and idea sharing allow us all to do better work.

Partner and group work allow children to practice their social skills. Collaboration is part of life and of being a community member. Collaboration can also be tricky. I like to have kids have a work meeting before embarking on collaborative work. A work meeting is a brief conversation that includes agreeing on an initial plan or concept, dividing work responsibilities and roles, and—this is big—deciding a custody arrangement for nonephemeral work. A custody arrangement establishes what will happen to the finished object once completed. Trust me, this is imperative and reduces conflict on the back end.

Collaboration can and will lead to conflict. Conflict isn't necessarily a bad thing. Conflict can simply mean that there's a problem to solve. Through collaborative build and play, children learn how to solve interpersonal problems, how to communicate their needs and desires, and how to compromise. Do your best to allow children to work through collaborative conflict on their own. If needed, interview and mirror each child's desires. Ask how each child is willing to compromise. We all want our children to have empathy for and work well with others while they maintain their own voice and boundaries. Collaborative creative work is the perfect space for children to practice these skills. Also, making things with people can be super fun.

Throughout this book, I offer suggestions on ways to collaborate with your children, how to have your children have a collaborative mind-set, and how to access the resources in your broader community.

3.

BE RESPONSIBLE FOR YOUR OWN SAFETY

When children are learning to be self-sufficient risk-takers, it's incredibly important that they're taught to be responsible for their own safety. We can support safe working practices with children through demonstration and modeling, and by giving gentle reminders. I have a good friend whose child was a runner. When he was young, around four years old, he would run out the front door of the shop every chance he got. His mother was frustrated by this behavior. He was a runner because he wasn't yet responsible for his own safety. His mother always protected him just before the danger of running became real to him. She asked for help. The next time he ran, we stopped him but also showed him the possible dangers he was facing when he ran (without being too harsh or scary). I got on his level and asked him to point to the places that were dangerous for him, such as the road. I asked him what would happen if we didn't stop him. He said, "I could get hurt." I asked him if he could stop himself in order to be safe. He paused, thought, and said yes. We told him he is now big enough to be safe for himself. He liked the idea of keeping himself safe. Now, this doesn't always work, and personal safety is largely dependent on a child's developmental stages. Children should be made aware of the risks of certain behaviors and allowed to assess and respond to as much risk as they're developmentally ready for. When we shield children from risk, they're actually less able to assess risk and make safe choices as they grow more independent. However, if we can meet kids where they're capable, give them as much responsibility as they can handle, and model safe working practices, they will organically do the things that shield them from harm.

4.

FAILURE IS AN OPTION

This is a big one! No one loves to fail. We're built to avoid failure. Our inherent fear of failure can keep us from taking chances and innovating, and ultimately our fears can keep us from succeeding. I like to say that the shop is failure-rich space. We make a lot of terrible things around here. As cocreators, we can model failure. Talk openly about all the times you tried something and failed. Model a "let's try it and see what happens" approach and your little ones will follow suit. If you have a perfectionist child (I have one), try to build small failures into everyday tasks. Impermanent practice can also help reduce this rigid success-or-fail mentality. This can look like deliberately making throwaway work or working with chalk, as it's easily erased.

I talk openly about what we do when things don't work out. I will tell the kids that I like to throw my work on the floor, tear it up, and generally freak out. This always gets a laugh, and the kids will tell me all the strategies they have to overcome frustration and disappointment. They take a deep breath, ask for help, take a break, start over, and so on. Little people are so smart! Failure lets us know that we're trying. Try to develop a practice for reflecting on failure without dwelling on all the things gone wrong.

HERE ARE SOME QUESTIONS ABOUT FAILURE TO ASK KIDS:

- What felt hard?
- What did you do about it?
- Why didn't that go like you imagined?
- What changes would help?
- How were you feeling when you made this?
- What did you learn?
- What skills do you need to develop to be more successful next time?

"Oh, look! Is that a giraffe?" when they've worked all day on a sculpture of a dog.

Here are some open ended-questions and questioning statements for children, caregivers, and collaborators:

WHAT IS YOUR PLAN?

- Tell me about your work.
- What was your biggest struggle?
- What are you most proud of?
- What would you do differently?
- Tell me about this detail.
- The biggest question of all: What else is possible?

5.

ASK A LOT OF QUESTIONS

Asking questions is how we grow. Questioning is at the core of creativity and learning. Often, children have learned that asking questions can make them feel stupid and vulnerable. As caregivers, we can all get fatigued by the endless questions that children pose on a daily basis. If we can encourage questioning, no matter how seemingly silly, we encourage a growth mind-set, one where knowledge-seeking and collaboration is celebrated. Questioning happens in two directions: the questions we ask children and the questions we want children to ask of themselves and their work. I often see parents ask questions that inadvertently deflate children. Open-ended questions are the types of questions that allow the child to reflect on their work rather than to assess the "goodness" or accuracy of their work. Do your best not to guess about what a child has created. Nothing takes the wind out of a kid's sail like hearing,

6.

GET A SECOND SET OF EYES ON YOUR WORK

Again, collaboration is at the core of being a successful maker. We collaborate through the feedback process as well as when work is cocreated. Don't be afraid to ask for feedback. Shared feedback helps us grow. We can model giving and seeking feedback by giving specific suggestions and by removing approving/disapproving remarks, such as "I like it" or "I don't like it." Feedback should be given when solicited, or ask first, "Can I give you a suggestion . . . ?" "What if . . . ?" is a great way to start a collaborative feedback session, as it's ultimately up to the maker to implement feedback.

I seem to always have a finisher in my class, that one kid who is done within five minutes. Here's where you can utilize the feedback process to push children to work a little harder, to consider a little more. When a finisher pops up with an "I'm done!" I ask them to ask three kids for suggestions. The finisher can ask the others, "What else is possible?" The finisher can choose to modify their work based on the suggestions or not. It's up to the maker to accept feedback. Usually it gets them started on a new line of detail or embellishment.

7.

FIND AN EXPERT; FOLLOW THEIR LEAD

We're all about learning from experts around here. Following the lead of an expert doesn't mean that you have to copy the work of others. It simply means that we should be open to the expertise and experiences of others who have traveled the path before us. Seek out those in your community who know something about what you want to know about.

Here at the shop, we have the luxury of working with master craftspeople all the time. We bring in people from all walks of life to share their skills. Look for community events that allow your kids to interact with people who have a depth of knowledge that you may not have. Maker fairs happen all over the world. Open studios and events that include historic reenactments are great ways for kids to engage with community experts. As parents and teachers, we can't know it all.

8.

CRAFTSMANSHIP IS AS MUCH ABOUT THE PROCESS AS PRODUCT

We're so often focused on the outcome, the product of our work. When we think of craftsmanship as a set of working practices, we can get to successful products naturally. Craftsmanship can often be conflated with perfection. Craftsmanship, to me, is really more about how we work to get to a desired product. We must first learn to work in ways that enable our success. Throughout this book I offer a variety of strategies that focus on the process of being a maker. Practices such as playfulness, trial and error, and planning help us produce our best work organically. Kids are inherently process focused, especially at early ages.

9.

CLEAN UP YOUR MESSES (LITERALLY AND FIGURATIVELY)

I can't stress enough the benefits of letting kids clean up their own messes. We all make mistakes, spill things, and break things. Children of all ages can learn to be responsible for their own messes. We have a shop rule that no one leaves with their work until they've helped clean up. It's a simple ask but with profound implications. Children learn that they're part of a community and that they're responsible to the people around them and the spaces they inhabit.

We also model problem solving. We all make messes of our personal relationships sometimes, and it can feel hard to admit that you've made a mistake, that you may have caused hurt to another person. Cleaning up messes can also look like admitting when you've hurt someone. As adults, we can model the cleanup process by apologizing when we've been hurtful and offering a solution to the problem. It can be hard for anyone to stop, go back, and set things right. If we start as children, we're more likely to develop the wherewithal to take care of our environment and our relationships.

10.
BE RESPONSIBLE TO YOURSELF AND YOUR SHOPMATES

Being responsible to yourself and your shopmates encompasses many of the working processes above. When we work together, we're responsible for being positive contributors. We're each responsible for carrying our own weight. I will discuss ways to develop working rules and practices that collectively will serve as a road map for responsible behaviors in the workshop space.

Being responsible to yourself and your shopmates is really all about kindness and respect. If you say you're going to do something, do it. We build trust with children based on our actions. When we model personal responsibility, children learn to be responsible for their words and actions. For the child, this can look like, again, doing what you say you will,

engaging with others with kindness and positivity, cleaning up, collaborating, and coming to the space ready to work.

11.
GO SLOW, HAVE FUN: IT'S ALL ABOUT THE PROCESS

I coined this phrase when we were developing our soap carving kits and it's stuck with me. *Go slow* is a gentle reminder that we don't need to rush through to the end product. *Have fun* reminds us to engage positively and playfully. *It's all about the process* reminds us that to truly be craftspeople, we must be process-oriented. Although the process can be messy, we clean it up. The process is meant to be enjoyable, and for children especially, as important as the outcome.

12.
PEOPLE WORK BEST IN BEAUTIFUL AND FUNCTIONAL SPACE

I will expand on the concept of beautiful and functional spaces in the following section, but at its most simple core, we all deserve to work in spaces that we find inspiring and functional. It's hard for anyone to do their best work in spaces that feel dilapidated and disorganized. A thoughtfully created, beautiful, and functional work space is the container for us to create our best work.

REFLECTION

Though not part of the Shop Model per se, after an action-packed day of making things at the shop, we like to take a moment to share and reflect on our work. So often, we work hard to complete a task, finish, and move on. But what if we all paused a little more often to reflect? Reflection allows us to refine our practices and solidify our learning. Reflection also allows us as facilitators to model process-oriented thinking.

Artists learn to refine and reflect through critiques. The word *critique* can often lead to feelings of inadequacy, that we're pointing out the negatives. However, with the right language and framing, the critique process becomes a time to reflect on the process and find the gems—even if those gems are ways in which we will work differently next time we tackle a creative task. Here are a few ways to reflect with kids.

QUESTIONING

Questioning puts the process into the hands of the maker. Here are some questions to pose to your child.

WHAT WENT WELL?

° What would you do differently next time?

° Where did you struggle?

° What problems did you face?

° What did you do to solve the problem?

° What are you most proud of?

NOTICING

Noticing gives an outside perspective on the maker's work. Be careful not to nitpick or focus on the negatives. Remember that specific, positive feedback is best. Improvements can be framed as positive inquiries. The choice to make changes, to refine a piece, or to try a new strategy should be made by the maker, regardless of age.

° I notice _____.

° What if _____?

° I tried this strategy and it worked really well. Would you like me to show you?

Refer to these practices as your makers learn and grow. You may notice a need or desire to focus on one or more of these practices at a time. If you're working with a larger group of kids, emphasis may begin on the more collaborative processes. If you're setting up a home workshop space, an emphasis on the personal and space-driven practices may be more beneficial. No matter which parts and pieces of the Shop Model speak to you, at the core the Shop Model includes simply practices for being aware of how we work and the spaces we choose to work in.

CREATING AND MAINTAINING
A SPACE FOR MAKING

One of my teaching mentors used to always say, "Start as you'd like to proceed." Starting as you'd like to proceed is all about thoughtful preparation, seeing the end result of your practice, and creating the container for certain outcomes to take place. When I was a teacher, I had four different classrooms, all with different advantages and disadvantages. The disadvantages: some of my classrooms had broken heat, no AC, leaky roofs, not enough chairs, broken tables, and no exterior windows. The advantages: wall space, sinks, worktables, lighting, a kiln (certainly to the dreamiest advantage). Whatever the physical advantages or disadvantages of your work space, and no matter your budget, a little thoughtful preparation can go a long way.

As a companion to a Navy man or as a child of the Great Depression, my grandmother was the ultimate creator of space and home, no matter where she lived. She learned to always iron and put up the curtains first, unpack the boxes, and make a home. If you have space, claim it, use what you have, live in it from day one. It will always change and evolve, but if you start as you'd like to proceed, the space will become activated, usable, and lively.

When I create creative spaces for kids, I begin by thinking about the space I have, including all of the advantages and disadvantages. I then make a list (I love a good list) of all the ways I or my client would like to use the space. In other words, how do we see ourselves proceeding in the space? From a classroom to a craft corner in your home, here are a few basic principles that will enable children to work and create effectively in a space.

INCLUDE THE KIDS

If at all possible, developing a work space for children should involve the children who will inhabit and use the space. When children are enlisted to cocreate their work space—works to organize, add, and place materials—they're better able to take ownership and responsibility for their space and the materials within it. It can be enticing to set up shop when the children are away or sleeping. I encourage you to take the slow route. Make a project of it. Children as young as two or three can help with the process. Children can help organize and sort, choose elements, and even create labels and signage. Just as with all things we create, we take more ownership when we've played a part in making it happen.

USE WHAT YOU HAVE

Begin by sorting what you have. Pull out all of your craft materials and sort your current collection of items. Discard the unusable items. (But save those marker lids!) Donate what you won't use. Save what truly speaks to you and your children. These are the items your children will actually use within the next few months. Maybe you have tons of fabric, but your children show little interest in fiber crafts; save a bit and discard the stockpile. This will allow you to make room for items that spark interest.

Chances are, you have more materials and tools than you think you do. I like to begin by sorting all the materials and supplies I already have into containers that are easy to access. If you have large

amounts of materials, you can portion them into small project-sized containers and save the rest in clear bins for future projects. This will enable you and the kids to thoughtfully use materials rather than use all of something without purpose. You will also be able to take a running inventory of what you currently have and develop a shopping list of items to acquire. It's not necessary to have every craft item all at once, although, I don't know about you, but any excuse to accumulate more craft goodness is one I'll take. Be creative and use what you've got. You can then be more thoughtful about what you choose to purchase and acquire.

Identify a primary storage area. This may be shelves or a movable caddy. Stock the items you already own. You'll then be able to clearly see what you have room for. Depending on the size of your creative space, you will need to be thoughtful about what stays, what goes, and what you bring in. The last thing you want in a creative space is too much clutter. Children (all people) work best in well-organized and simple spaces.

If you have space, look for a secondary storage area. This is where you can tuck away overflow items in clear plastic bins or whatever you have, really. It's a good idea to clearly label your storage containers, lest you forget what's inside and miss an opportunity to use it. If your children are writing, have them help create the labels. Even preliterate children can draw images of the items inside each container. By having a secondary storage area, you will be better equipped to rotate in new items. This periodically reactivates the space. This also allows you to store items that require adult supervision, such as power tools.

Choose your work surface. This may very well be your dining table. In order to preserve your work surface, have a roll of paper, mats, or a drop cloth available. Placing a covering on the table can also signify a shift in use. If you're using your dining table and would like to continue to also use it to eat and gather, you can develop setup and cleanup practices that include storing materials back on shelves and clearing the table covering at the end of every maker session. For smaller friends, I've had great luck on resale websites finding funky vintage kids' furniture that suits my aesthetic and can be resold as children grow into the space. Again, no need to buy a custom workbench here. Take a cue from the Montessori environment: a thoughtfully placed mat on the floor can be an ideal maker surface. In fact, many of our shop kids prefer to work on the floor, as it

allows them to spread out and move their bodies organically.

STOCK WITH ITEMS YOUR CHILD(REN) CAN USE IN A VARIETY OF WAYS

It can be enticing to spend lots of money to outfit a creative space. Don't do it! Being resourceful is all parts of the creative practice for adults and for kids. As an art teacher, I had years where I was given $1.50 per kid, per year, to purchase supplies, and I made it work. Project-specific tools and materials are great, and if your children show substantial interest, invest in those items. I would, however, start with materials and supplies that can be used in a variety of ways. Some of my favorite supplies are completely free and teach kids the valuable lesson of reusing items destined for the landfill.

Here's a punch list of my top consumable maker supplies in order of expense.

FREE

We can teach children from a young age to use items that would otherwise be discarded as their primary resources for creative play. Being resourceful and ecological are all great lessons to learn early.

- Cardboard, cardboard, cardboard! Process it down for usable platforms and shapes. Cut it up using a paper cutter or box cutter. Save tubes and cereal boxes.
- Bottle caps and corks. Keep a jar in your kitchen to collect caps and cool plastic items.

- Paper. Save interesting paper goods. Sort and remove cut-up pieces periodically.

- Yarn and fabric scraps. How are these free? Jump on your local neighborhood board and ask for it! Chances are, your neighbors have an overflow of materials to share.

- Wood scraps. Get scrappin'! Scour your alleys or neighborhood for discarded wood or check the remnant bins for deeply discounted scrap wood. At most large hardware stores, you can ask to have them cut the wood into manageable pieces for a small fee. Just make sure that you don't use pressure-treated wood with children. It's treated with toxic chemicals.

- Sticks of all shapes and sizes. What child doesn't love to collect? Head out on a walk to collect fallen sticks and interesting natural objects, such plants, acorns, rocks, and leaves. Just be sure to ask permission before foraging. Find expanded notes on foraging in the "Heritage Skills" section.

DOLLAR STORE ITEMS

We like to use as many sustainable resources as possible; however, there are a variety of craft staples that are available at your local dollar store.

- Pom-poms
- Popsicle sticks
- Pipe cleaners
- Clothespins
- Googly eyes
- Small rocks
- Moss
- Beads
- Buttons

- Markers
- Pencils
- Foam sheets
- Raffia
- Hole punch
- Brads
- Rubber bands
- Tweezers
- Artificial flowers

CRAFT STORE STAPLE ITEMS

There are a few staple items that can be purchased at your local craft store that I like to keep on hand for all-purpose making.

- Low-temp hot glue gun
- Glue-gun sticks
- 2 good pairs of scissors: 1 for paper, 1 for fabric
- Felt sheets
- No. 18 sharp embroidery needles
- Plastic needles
- Embroidery floss
- Elmer's Glue-All glue (good glue is worth the extra few cents)
- Permanent markers
- Paint: tempera cakes, tempera sticks
- Paintbrushes
- Small wood parts
- Foam pieces

HARDWARE STORE

This is the short list for small spaces where power tools and sawdust may not be an option. Invest in adult-sized tools that function for small hands. Most children's tools on the market are less than effective and actually less safe than the adult options. (Flip forward to the "Woodworking" section for a dream shop list.)

- Small safety glasses (toss them in the dishwasher to disinfect)
- Hammer
- Nails
- Screwdriver
- Screws
- Sandpaper
- Nuts and bolts for loose parts (also may be found for free via community request)
- Scrap wood

OTHER

- Canvas rugs
- Aprons/work shirts
- Kid-sized leather work gloves
- Rags/washcloths
- Child-sized broom and dustpan
- Containers: jars, trays, baskets, boxes, clear plastic bins
- Trash and recycling bins

ORGANIZE AND MAINTAIN THE SPACE

Let's be honest, aesthetics matter. The way we plan, organize, and decorate a space creates the container for work to take place. If we don't pay attention to our working environment, we lose something of the creative process. Clutter, mess,

and lack of attention to detail can doom a potentially creative space to become a messy dormant one. But not to worry! It's not necessary to spend all of your days on Instagram and Pinterest, pining away for the perfect creative space. Every space will be different, and it's up to you to design it to work best for you and your kids. By focusing on a few guiding principles, anyone can develop a beautiful and functional work space.

A work space for children need not be filled with primary colors, characters, and plastic. Children often function better in simple, soothing spaces. Spaces that are free from unnecessary clutter and stimuli allow children the room to imagine and create without distraction. Choose shelving, storage, and work surfaces that speak to your aesthetic and the spaces you've established for your adult self.

Organize materials into easily accessible containers for materials for daily use. I prefer to use containers made of natural materials for the primary presentation. I love to reuse jars, and thrift stores are typically overrun with baskets of all shapes and sizes. A wooden tray with small compartments makes a perfect presentation for small parts. Items for everyday use should be placed at an accessible level for small hands. Only put out the materials you want children to have easy access to. Materials can be organized into material sections. On our supply shelves at the shop we have sections for fiber materials, cardboard, tinker and small parts, woodworking, drawing and painting, and finally, natural materials. There are no hard-and-fast rules here; materials

will be and should be used for a variety of purposes. Sectioning helps children envision the work and material options that are available. Also, it becomes easier to give a provocation based on materials. For example, let's create using only natural materials today. Or, what can you create using cardboard, brads, and a hole punch?

As a reminder, project-specific and more expensive materials and tools should be stored away in the secondary storage area, in a cabinet or up out of reach. As you develop working practices, you will establish rules and norms for how these secondary materials are accessed.

Create caddies for tools of the trade. A wire basket can be filled with basic art supplies such as scissors, glue, markers, pencils, and so forth. Use another basket or a toolbox (page 98) to store woodworking tools and supplies. It's a good idea to keep the hot glue gun separate and to create an expectation that an adult knows when a hot glue gun is coming out.

CREATE RULES FOR YOUR CREATIVE SPACE

Believe it or not, kids love rules. Rules help kids to understand how things work. Rules help us do our best work. When I cocreate rules or expectations with kids, I make sure to elicit positive rule creation rather than a list of things not to do. We make a short list of ways of being—of the yeses. Rituals and routines actually enable children to be more creative and spontaneous because the container, the boundaries, are explicit. They know how to flex and move within the creative space without spilling over into chaos.

An old teacher trick is to use the "looks like, sounds like, feels like" method. This enables children as young as three to identify ways in which simple rules and expectations are carried out within a space and within the different parts of the work cycle. Here's a simple script we use at the shop to quickly and effectively establish working practices with kids.

GROWN-UP: All spaces have rules, don't they? What rules do you think we should have for this space?

KIDS: Don't run! Don't hit.

GROWN-UP: So we should be safe? Should that be a rule?

KIDS: Yes!

GROWN-UP: Okay, great. What does that look like, sound like, and feel like? [*Write down the responses in a list.*]

GROWN-UP: What is another rule we should have?

KIDS: Don't be mean!

GROWN-UP: So we should be kind? Should that be a rule? How can we be kind to one another and the space? What does that look like, sound like, and feel like when we're getting started, working, and when we're done with our work?

Drive the conversation about how to approach the work space with kindness. This can look like modeling and practicing how we get our materials, how we work without excessive mess, how we clean up. It should always be the expectation that children clean up their own messes (more about this in working practices).

GROWN-UP: Are there any other rules we should have?

KIDS: Have fun!

Making is and should be a pleasurable act. Having fun looks all sorts of ways, and in the creative space, we like to remind kids that fun looks a bit different than it does on the playground. It's calm, in control, and often quiet.

A great first project for your new space is to create a sign listing the new rules and expectations using the supplies and space within the new rules. This activity allows the children to model and practice working behaviors in a mindful way. For preliterate kiddos, they can draw a picture for each practice.

As your children begin to work within their new space, review the rules as needed, give praise, and notice when children are demonstrating kind behavior or safe use of tools and materials. Praise and noticing go much further than criticism and consequence.

KEEP IT CLEAN

It's often a challenge to get kids to stop working when you need them to. (What a problem to have!) When I was an art teacher, I had the daily challenge to get upward of thirty kids in and out of my classroom every forty-five minutes, with two minutes between each group. You have to be a cleanup master in that kind of environment! Here's what I've learned about cleaning up with kids.

Practice your cleanup routine explicitly. Be incredibly clear with your instructions.

If you want them to put all the markers away with the lids on facing up, practice it! If you want all the materials in the correct bins, practice it. Practices become rituals and routines through consistent repetition, and bad habits are hard to break. Again, praise and notice when they're following through. A simple statement such as "You're a cleanup master! We'll be able to work longer next time!" reinforces clean up practices.

I've used the same cleanup routine with kids, more or less, for fifteen years. Here's how it goes.

Start by giving work-time reminders. Kids like to know, even if time is still abstract, how much time they have to work. Give a five-minute warning that work time will be over. Give another prompt at one minute: "Next time you hear my voice, it will be time to clean up." Next, get the kids' attention. This can look like a consistent signal that you've established. I use "Show me ten fingers high in the sky." (This makes the kids have to stop working with both hands.) "Eyes on me." Once you have the children's attention, give your cleanup instructions. Give no more than three directions at a time, especially for younger kids. I usually have kids put their work away, then materials, then sweep/wipe tables. Again, this is a great time for noticing and narration. Noticing and narration is a practice that enables the caregiver to give praise and to solidify desired behaviors without attaching the notion that children should perform for the acceptance or favor of adults. For instance, a narration can sound like "You're a cleanup machine!" or "Look how nicely you put those materials away." This type of narration sounds very different than caregiver-pleasing language, such as "I like how Charlie swept so quickly" or "I love how Susy wiped down the table."

However, careful redirection and logical consequences are completely reasonable. Not ready to be safe with hot glue? Simply remove it and say, "We'll try this again in a few days." A child may naturally protest when you set limits. We've all experienced a tantrum, a grumpy face, a little back talk. And I know as a parent this can feel much harder to follow through with when they're your own, but it's okay for kids to struggle with boundaries. It's okay to say no to a child who isn't being safe, who isn't taking care of their things, who just might not be ready for new materials, a tool, or a privilege. It's okay to try, fail, and try again, both for us as caregivers and for our kids. That's modeling kindness. Kindness is knowing our own limits and learning to respect the limits of others.

TIP: *I take a cue from the Montessori world and always have 2 x 3 roll-up canvas rugs available as versatile and washable work surfaces. These rugs help contain the mess to a work zone and enable children to work at a table or on the floor.*

MAINTAINING AN ACTIVE SPACE

In my creative life, I've seen numerous spaces live and die. What I've learned about creating a creative space that you and children will use regularly is that it needs to feel alive, to be in your everyday

view, in your everyday life. It needs to suit your desires in a way that works for you. And just as we develop rituals and routines while we use the space, it may be beneficial to schedule your work time at first, to build into your rhythms and routines the time for making, exploring, and playing in your work space. It absolutely does not need to be a huge, separate space from your everyday life. When I was very little, my mom would set up crafts on an old mossy picnic table just outside our kitchen window. My brother and I would spend hours in that little side yard making and playing while my mom kept a watchful eye from the window. When my oldest son, Milo, was three, Jon bought me a beautiful old drafting table off of Craigslist and set up a small studio space in our teeny-tiny sunroom. In just seventy square feet, Milo and I would spend hours each day painting and making. Some of the best maker spaces are tucked in right next to the dining table, where most of our daily lives happen.

Once the space begins to feel stagnant or you notice the kids being drawn to work less and less, it's time to change things. As much as I love a good routine, change is inevitable, change is good, and change can lead to great work. Change out materials periodically, add tools and supplies as your children's interests change and as they get older.

As you use and develop your space, maintenance becomes an important factor in keeping your work space lively. We all clean out our kitchen cupboards and closets every so often. The same type of maintenance keeps your work space from becoming cluttered and full of half-finished projects and used materials. Your regular cleanup routine should keep things relatively organized, but things tend to build up. Every so often, in collaboration with the children who use the space, go through all materials and work. Toss unusable materials and supplies and make a list of things that need to be restocked. Resort bins and supplies. Dust and wipe down containers and surfaces. Taking care of our tools and materials is an integral part of the maker process and teaches children to value and care for their things.

The million-dollar question: What to do with all those cool creations? Making stuff leads to stuff that's been made. What do you do with all of those creations, especially if you're short on space? My youngest son, Wyatt, is a prolific maker. He spends hours at the shop each week and has produced so many cool things. Also, he tends to be a bit of a hoarder. Periodically we have a sort. I will set a limit to the number of handmade items he may keep or a goal of how many items we can exit from his room. Having a number seems to help avoid the trappings of begging and negotiating, especially with little ones. We sort handmade items into three categories: keep, give, and toss. This is the same rule that many folks use when they're purging household items, except when we give, we give the handmade item as a thoughtful gift (with the implied intention that the recipient needn't keep it for a lifetime). Kept items will either be on display or used as toys. For the very special item, it may find its way into Wyatt's keepsake box. For the toss, we disassemble and return what we can to the supply bins, recycle what can be recycled, and toss the rest. There's no perfect system to combat the accumulation of made items. Do what works for you and your kids. But if we can work to develop an attitude of letting go, of giving, of process over product, we're less likely to be weighed down by our things.

Your creative space will ultimately be a reflection of you and your makers. Start with what you can, and your work space will develop and change over time. Collaborate, reflect, and change things as needed. Set aside time to sit in your space and reflect on how it's being used. Be willing to change what isn't working and celebrate what is working. At the end of the day, your work space should bring you and your makers joy, not stress. And please, don't worry if it's not Instagram/Pinterest perfect.

PART ONE

HERITAGE SKILLS

Heritage skills are crafts and practices that connect us to our human history. These activities will encourage children to slow down and understand the technologies that brought us to our current day, all while encouraging children to develop self-sufficiency. These five projects allow children to see themselves as independent and capable, as caregivers of their environment, and as part of the fabric of our collective past.

In this first chapter, we will start at the beginning. These projects will enable you and your kids to actively think about and connect to our shared past by making and creating in the natural world. I will discuss how we see human innovation and shared culture, how we connect to the plants growing around us, and perhaps most importantly, how we encourage kids to slow down just enough to be thoughtful and reflective risk-takers, problem-solvers, and self-sufficient humans.

ONE

SHELTER BUILDING

Along with food and water, shelter is a basic human need. There's no better place to start on our maker path than with shelter building. I've yet to meet a child who doesn't love building forts of all shapes and materials. In fact, I spent a good portion of the summer between second and third grade reading books in a tastefully decorated cardboard refrigerator box. There are safety and security in shelter, and there's something ingrained in humans to seek safety and security, to create protective spaces.

We all live in different environments—rural, city, desert, and so on. How we relate to those environments matters. Most children and adults can identify only a handful of trees and plants in their surroundings. So often we exist in space without knowing it. We can use shelter building as an entry point into conversations about how humans interact with the environment.

In his 1914 book *Shelters, Shacks, and Shanties*, D. C. Beard, the founder of the Boy Scouts of America, often talks about the history of shelter, from an immediate, primal need to the creation of permanent structure, creating place. I've always admired his "just for the fun of it" approach and the trust he placed in young people to be able to build complex structures and objects. Skill building is fun. Learning to do hard things is fun. Making things big and small to play with is just fun. Although his work is firmly rooted in the thoughts and practices of its time, his sentiments, when applied, can benefit kids from all walks of life.

Sit Spot

Before we build shelters, we sit, we notice. We sit where our shelter is meant to be constructed and feel the light on our face, the breeze on our skin; we smell the earth below us and the air around us; we observe the insects crawling on the ground. We notice the world around us. We wonder.

My kids picked their first sit spots on my grandparents' land when they were three and five. My oldest just so happened to have chosen my favorite spot to sit when I was a child—a sunny little rock that overlooks the meadow. This is a place in the world they continue to return to season after season. The view changes, the trees fall, the animals change, the kids change. The place is the same.

During our Ancestral Skills camps, we have kids choose "sit spots" for the week. We start with five minutes, and by the end of the week, kids as young as five are sitting for twenty minutes in silence, noticing the world around them with all five senses entirely turned on. The first sit can be an anxious time for a child. They don't often have to sit with "nothing" to do for even five minutes. It's okay if they wiggle. It's okay if they get distracted and chase butterflies. (I'm thinking of you, Virginia!) There should be no force applied to this activity but rather a slow settling into the act of listening and observing. We've had great success with a simple timer and a few words of encouragement.

There are endless variations on a simple stick shelter. I will outline our three favorites here, but really, exploration and creative problem-solving is the primary goal.

Who's it for?

➤ Best for kids ages 4+

➤ Adaptable for kids as young as 2½

Time Commitment

➤ 1 hour to days on end

Mess Level

➤ Sawdust, sticks, and maybe some mud

What You Need

➤ Outdoor space

➤ Y-shaped sticks are a super score

➤ A whole mess of 4-foot-long (or longer) sticks

OPTIONAL

➤ *Saw and twine*

➤ *Leaves and small sticks, debris*

➤ *Bedsheets, blankets, or old clothes*

TIP: No access to nature? Bring it inside with ½-inch dowels or bamboo, string, and good old-fashioned bedsheets.

Safety Tips

➤ Make sure that the structure is stable before entering.

➤ Safety glasses and work gloves are good calls when working with sticks.

A-FRAME SURVIVAL SHELTER

The A-frame survival shelter is one of the quickest and easiest shelter forms. It's relatively quick to construct and provides a warm shelter in a pinch.

1. Gather 2 Y-shaped sticks for legs and 1 long stick to act as the spine of the structure (known as the ridgepole). The Y-shaped sticks should be long enough to allow a child to crawl inside, and the ridgepole should be a bit longer than your child is tall. Stand the Y-shaped sticks at an angle toward each other with the crooks of the sticks facing toward each other. Feed the ridgepole through the Ys of the sticks and push together until the Ys hold the ridgepole firmly in place.

2. The other end of the ridgepole should be ground into the earth a bit for stability. This will create a descending angle from the top of the Y-shaped sticks into the ground.

3. Line the walls of the framework with smaller sticks like the ribs of a rib cage. If available, leaves and debris can be piled on the frame to keep out wind, rain, and sun.

CONICAL TENT

We often think of the tepee and Native Americans when we think of this iconic cone-shaped structure. However, the conical tent was used by nomadic people throughout the world for thousands of years. In Sweden, it's the *lavvu*. The Uralic people from Siberia created the *chum*; and the Finnish had the *goahti*, a slightly shorter, squatter version of the traditional design. What all of these structures have in common is a circular, straight-pole construction with an opening at the top to provide exhaust from internal fires. The structure is relatively easy to construct and take down, retains heat, and provides ample shelter from the elements. A conical tent also requires fewer sticks to forage and can be created from bamboo garden stakes or dowels.

1. Using 6–8 sticks at least 4 feet in length, lash the sticks together at the top.

2. Fan the bottom of the sticks out in a circular pattern on the ground to steady the structure.

3. Cover the shelter. Here's where you and the kids can get really creative. What materials are available to insulate the shelter? More sticks like our A-frame? Bedsheets? Blankets? Old clothes? Bark?

LEAN-TO

This one requires finding a sweet spot in the natural world. A lean-to requires finding 2 trees that will act as the braces for the overall structure. The hunt for the perfect spot can feel like a treasure hunt!

1. Find 2 trees a few feet apart from each other that have branches at a similar height.

2. Settle a ridgepole into the crux of the tree branches, creating a horizontal beam.

3. Lay sticks (the ribs) diagonally from the ridgepole to the ground to build the roof of the structure.

4. Embellish as you like. I've seen kids work on lean-to structures for days on end, adding walls and thatching, and creating a cozy interior.

Guiding Questions

➤➤ What makes a structure strong and sturdy?

➤➤ How can we be safe while trying new things?

➤➤ How can we look to the natural environment to provide for our needs?

Extensions

FOR EVERYONE

Make mini shelters. When we don't have ample materials, we gather small sticks and make shelters for stuffies and woodland creatures.

FOR KIDS AGES 4 AND UNDER / DELAYED MOTOR SKILLS

With more adult assistance, the focus can be on the play that occurs within the shelter. Pretend play, and the feeling of warmth and shelter, can be the focus.

FOR KIDS AGES 8 AND UP / ADVANCED MOTOR AND CREATIVE SKILLS

Make a shelter that will last four seasons. What do you need to reinforce the structure?

TWO

SOAP CARVING

One of our favorite pastimes at the shop is carving soap with a homemade wooden knife. When I was ten and my cousin Tony was sixteen, he taught me how to whittle a stick in our backyard. Tony was (and is always) a careful and patient teacher, making sure that I knew the dangers and rewards of safely using any tool. Flash forward to the first days of our shop, and he once again showed me how to safely use knives with children. One of our first camps ever, he was whittling with real bushcraft knives and using wooden knives with younger kids. A knife is one of the most useful tools ever developed, and any bushcrafter will tell you that they wouldn't leave home without one.

Using knives and sharp tools with children can be intimidating. However, when we give proper attention to the introduction of tools, most hand tools are actually no more dangerous than scissors or pencils.

I Do, We Do, You Do

How do we know when our kids are ready for a task? It can be so challenging to identify exactly when to introduce a new tool or skill. There are some visible developmental milestones, but often it's about the individual child. In the education world, there's a concept that we learn best when a new skill or concept is just beyond what we already know. This is known as + 1. My mom would call this "moving fences." When children are very young, we protect them from the physical world. We swaddle. We carry. We babyproof. As children grow and mature, we gradually remove the barriers that keep them protected from potential harm. Sometimes as caregivers we keep those fences closed in for far too long, mostly because of our own fears. We see the potential risks and say, "No, thank you," to the potential that our child might fail or be physically hurt. It's our job as caregivers to keep kids safe. But at what cost? Our culture is increasingly challenging, yet we task adults to be bold and brave and big-world-problem-solvers. I often wonder how we expect kids to become adults with these inherent skills if we protect them from failure all of their childhoods.

We must allow children to find that +1 experience. Children can become fearful of risk because we fail to give them the opportunity to fall down, scrape a knee, and get back up. If children are kept entirely safe, wholly protected, they may lose the inner voice that allows them to assess risk independently, to create their own safety plans.

Whenever I introduce a new skill or material, I follow a simple procedure: I do,

we do, you do. If you're working one on one: I do, you do. I first ask what the child already knows about the material or tool. This allows children to bring in their prior knowledge as well as to dispel any misconceptions they may have. I then give any background information I might have that can deepen a child's connection to the craft. This can be anything from a personal story to a link to historical uses. For instance, soap carving with wooden knives has been a staple way of teaching knife skills to children for at least one hundred years, especially in rural Appalachia, where bar-soap making, as well as wooden toy making, have a rich history. Lastly, I demonstrate the desired skill. Check for understanding by having a child demonstrate the first parts of the task. This gradual-release practice allows us as caregivers to check for understanding and to build confidence in the abilities of the makers incrementally.

Soap carving is messy and fun. It provides a safe opportunity for kids to practice whittling and using a knife. In the beginning stages of learning knife skills, the knife should always point away from the user, making sure that the holding hand, legs, and other body parts aren't in the way of the direction of force being applied to the knife. Kids should be seated at a table or kneeling on the ground to keep those little legs out of the way!

A rustic wooden carving knife can be purchased from our website or whittled quickly from a stick. Even a slightly filed popsicle stick can do the trick. A soap boat is a classic first soap-carving project. We use Ivory soap as a carving block; it's easy to work with, it's inexpensive, and it floats.

Who's It For?

➤ Best for kids ages 4+

➤ Adaptable for ages 2½+

Time Commitment

➤ 30 minutes to 2 hours

Mess Level

➤ Get out a drop cloth and a broom!

➤ This is also a super-fun bath-time activity.

What You Need

➤ Drop cloth or tray

➤ A good old bar of Ivory soap

➤ Wooden knife, sharpened popsicle sticks, clay tools, and/or orange sticks

➤ Paper and toothpick for a sail

TIP: Got a kiddo who's sensitive to scents? Try an all-natural melt-and-pour soap base.

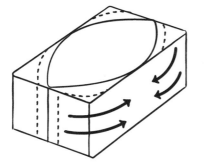

1. Put down a drop cloth or tray to contain the mess.

2. Use the template to carve your boat. Alternately, kids can draw a simple plan on the soap using a pencil or go free-form.

3. Using a knife or other wooden tools, demonstrate how to push the blade away from the child to take the material away. Go slow on this first demonstration. Show the angle of the tool as close to parallel with the surface of the soap. A good indicator of the proper carving technique is when a thin curl of soap forms as you take away material. (See illustration.)

4. For concave parts, like the inside of the boat, use the knife as a spoon to carefully scoop out the material a little bit at a time.

5. The knife can also be used to smooth the surface of the soap and to create lines and other details.

6. A simple sail can be created using a triangle cut from scrap paper. Cut or punch two holes, top and bottom, and thread a toothpick through as the mast.

Guiding Questions

➤ How do we stay safe when using sharp objects?

➤ What is the texture of the soap?

➤ What do you notice about the tools?

➤ How do you hold the knife or tool in your hand to get the best results?

➤ What do you do if the soap breaks?

➤ What do you do if it doesn't turn out the way you thought it would?

➤ Why does the soap float?

➤ What happens when your carving gets wet?

Extensions

FOR EVERYONE

➤ Use the wooden knife to scrape the bark of a fallen tree branch.

➤ Chop vegetables and fruit.

➤ Have a soap-boat race!

➤ Mash up your soap shavings to create a new sculpture.

FOR KIDS AGES 4 AND UNDER / DELAYED MOTOR SKILLS

➤ Hold the knife or tool together to help the child feel the pressure, angle, and motion of the carving.

➤ Little ones love to squish the soap shavings into all sorts of shapes.

➤ Pour water and shavings into a bowl or into the tub, mix, and see what happens!

➤ Cheese graters and most clay tools work well with the soap, too!

FOR KIDS AGES 8 AND UP / ADVANCED MOTOR AND CREATIVE SKILLS

➤ Soap carving can be taken to some very elevated levels! Think it and you can carve it out of soap. Check the resources list for books and websites with more advanced soap-carving patterns.

➤ At the shop, once a kiddo has demonstrated consistent, safe practices, we introduce carving knives and wood whittling. A child's first knife is a rite of passage, and we take it seriously. I asked my grandfather when he got his first knife, and he said he must have been four years old. In many cultures, children as young as two use large knives safely. This is a personal choice and one that you will make because you know your kid(s).

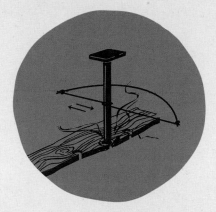

FIRE MAKING

As we learn how our ancestors survived and thrived without modern conveniences, we're able to help kids push through their restrictive ideas about doing hard things. Doing hard things can feel like friction inside the body. We feel uncomfortable when we're urged to accomplish hard things. That feeling just before we "get" it is when real learning and growth happens. It's said that the ability to create fire was the single most significant technological shift in human history. The use of fire is thought to be the catalyst for the growth of the human brain throughout nearly one million years. The ability to cook and process food through heat enabled humans to access energy from it more easily, thus increasing the mass of the human brain.

In addition to the physical changes that access to fire gave to humans, a fire is a symbol for the gathering place, the first classroom. The fire is a place in which people come together to share stories, learn skills, and build community.

In modern times, we tend to see fire from the point of view of danger, and for good reason. Wildfires and home fires are devastating. However, we can teach children to safely create and manage fire in a way that removes fear and encourages stewardship and responsibility. It doesn't hurt that fire making is inherently scientific and just plain cool.

If you've ever watched any popular survival show on television, even the most seasoned bushcraft expert can be challenged by the act of fire making. All of the pieces of the puzzle need to be just right to get the spark, the flame. That takes preparation, planning, effort, and adjustments along the way, and even then, there's still a chance for failure. If that isn't a perfect analogy for doing hard things, I don't know what is.

An Attitude of Play

When it comes to doing hard things, making a friction fire is up there on the list of hard things to learn and master. When we teach friction fire at our summer Maker Camps, we teach from an attitude of play. That may seem counterintuitive when working with fire. I'll explain. The attitude of play isn't one of reckless abandon but rather inquiry and discovery. It's process-oriented. If we as caregivers and teachers can model practice, failure, discovery, and work playfully, the process becomes as important as the outcome—especially considering, in this exercise, our lives don't depend on the ability to actually succeed in making fire. Modeling an attitude of play can look like struggling with a task while smiling and saying things such as "Oh, well. At least I'm having fun" or "I wonder how this is all going to go?"—all with a playful tone.

FIRE MAKING

There are a few ways to approach fire making with children. The top level is practicing friction fire with a traditional bow drill. Bow-drill fire making is a pan-global technology that dates back tens of thousands of years. The techniques are simple yet difficult to master. A bow-drill kit can be purchased online or created with a few necessary foraged materials. What I love about the bow drill is the simplicity of the machine. Friction is caused by spinning the bow drill against the fireboard. The friction then creates enough heat to create an ember; an ember with the help of oxygen becomes fire.

Often we start a discussion about fire making by simply lighting matches or seeing heat from the sun build through a magnifying glass. These two acts are simple ways of seeing how a chemical reaction (the match) and direct application of heat can cause a fire—all very exciting for our little ones.

Who's It For?
- Best for kids 6+

Time Commitment
- 20 minutes to 2 hours

Mess Level
- Take it outside.

What You Need

BOW-DRILL KIT
- Fireboard with notch
- Bow
- Spindle
- Socket
- Tinder/kindling

OPTIONAL
- Matches
- Magnifying glass

1. Create a loose tinder bundle large enough to fit in your hands using dry grasses, inner bark, or thinly shredded paper.

2. Place the fireboard on the ground. Use your left foot to hold it tightly to the ground.

FIREBOARD

READY TO NOTCH   BROKEN   NOTCHED

3. Wrap the bowstring around the spindle and place the spindle into the notch on the fireboard.

4. With your left hand, place the socket on top of the bow. Stabilize your left elbow with your right knee.

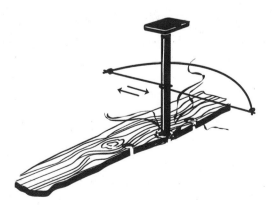

5. Using your right hand, pull the bowstring back and forth in a smooth motion. This will begin to create friction between the spindle and the fireboard. (See illustration.)

6. Once you get a good rhythm, you will create a small pile of ash that, with luck and perseverance, will lead to an ember.

EMBER

7. Once an ember (glowing red coal) is visible, transfer the ember quickly and carefully to your tinder bundle. (See illustration.)

8. Blow gently on the ember to ignite the tinder bundle.

Guiding Questions

➤ How does friction work?

➤ What are other ways to make fire?

➤ What causes heat?

➤ What safety precautions do we need to take?

Extensions

FOR EVERYONE
➤ Roast a marshmallow!

FOR KIDS AGES 4 AND UNDER / DELAYED MOTOR SKILLS
➤ Demonstrate how to make the friction fire.

➤ Have younger kids rub their hands together to create friction.

FOR KIDS AGES 8 AND UP / ADVANCED MOTOR AND CREATIVE SKILLS
➤ Have kids forage for and create their own bow-drill kit.

HERITAGE SKILLS

FOUR

BOWS AND ARROWS

The bow and arrow is a pan-global technology that seemingly developed independently in different places at similar times. Bows and arrows were primarily used as hunting tools but were also used as weapons. The act of shooting a bow is even used as meditative practice. Tools and practices from our collective past can often be ascribed to one group of people or one moment in time. The bow and arrow is one of those technologies that holds a cultural representation that may not be totally accurate. By understanding pan-global technologies and honoring their contributions to our collective past, we can better understand our shared human experience while honoring sacred practices of individual groups.

Building Cultural Awareness

A year or so after I started teaching art, I had the opportunity to spend the summer on a remote island off the coast of Juneau, Alaska, teaching art to Native kids from the Tlingit Nation. I had been inspired by and was teaching the symbolism of the Pacific Northwest tribes since my student teaching. Fifteen years ago, multiculturalism in arts education looked like imitating the art of other cultures without much regard for sacred traditions. A day or so into my contract, I was invited to come to the workshop of a community artisan. He showed me the totem pole he was carving and talked to me about the sacred traditions and how the Tlingit people owned the symbolism. I was struck by this. Culture is a movable and changing thing. It isn't static, and it's a challenge to understand the boundaries of using and creating certain practices, skills, tools, and symbols. However, when teaching and learning about craft traditions, it's easy to fall into a space that feels like cultural appropriation. Cultural appropriation is the adoption of elements of a minority culture by members of the dominant culture. This practice has roots in colonialism and the fetishization of indigenous people and traditions. In the case of my former teaching practices, I was appropriating and fetishizing the sacred symbols of the Pacific Northwest indigenous people. I intended to teach children about another culture; this isn't a bad idea. Cultural exchange is real and what helps humans grow, change, and evolve. But that exchange must be thoughtful and equitable. I recently heard the term *humble guest*. If we can come from a place of being a humble guest in the skill sharing and exploration of practices that are held in the tradition of cultures from which we don't originate, we're able to remove old patterns, to listen, to seek permission, and to be open.

BOW AND ARROW

When we shoot bows with kids, we talk about the different uses for this tool. We talk about the ways in which we would use a bow and arrow. We certainly don't want to create weapons, and I avoid creating play weapons with children. Our bows are for target practice only.

Who's It For?

►► Best for kids ages 8+

Time Commitment

►► 2 to 3 hours

Mess Level

►► Sawdust

What You Need

FOR THE ARROW (MAKES 1)

►► One ¼-inch-diameter straight stick or dowel, 16–18 inches long

►► 3 feathers

►► 1 yard sinew or waxed string

►► Glue

►► Drill and ¼-inch drill bit

►► 1 cork

►► Scissors

►► Saw

OPTIONAL

►► Paint

►► Paintbrushes

FOR THE BOW

►► ¼- to ½-inch-diameter greenwood or willow stick (Ikea), 28 inches long

►► 36-inch piece thin paracord or nylon string

►► Waxed string

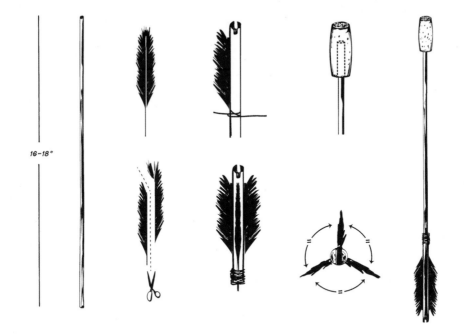

16-18"

MAKE THE ARROWS

1. Cut a ¼-inch notch on one end of the dowel; this is the nock.

2. Prepare the feathers. For each of the 3 feathers, cut away the feathers along the spine, leaving about ½ inch of the spine exposed at the bottom. Create a diagonal cut at the top of each feather.

3. Tie the sinew to the dowel (shaft) with a single slipknot.

4. Attach the feathers by holding 1 feather with the shaft against the dowel and the feather pointing away from the shaft. It will want to lay down as you wind the sinew around the shaft of the feather and the dowel. Be sure to hold the feather in

position (a little dab of hot glue can go far here). After 3 tight wraps, add another feather ⅓ of the way around the shaft, wind 3 times, add the final feather in the same way, and wrap 3 more times. Using the tail ends of the sinew, tie a square knot and trim the remaining sinew.

TIP: A quick pass of a lit match over the knot and a press of the fingers will melt a bit of the wax and seal the knot securely in place.

5. Drill a hole halfway into the cork. Push the dowel into the cork.

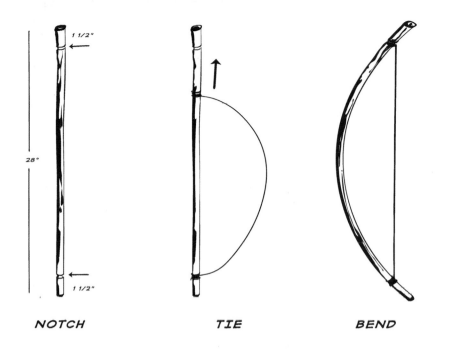

NOTCH   **TIE**   **BEND**

MAKE THE BOW

1. Create 1 notch about ⅛-inch deep all the way around either end of the stick, about 1½–2 inches from either end.

2. On one end of the stick tie the paracord or nylon string securely into the notch. Flip the bow and pull the string up along the length of the bow.

3. Tie the loose end of the string around the stick about 3 inches below the second notch. Make sure the knot is loose enough to slide up and down the stick. Slide the string to sit securely in the notch. This will bend the bow and create tension. It may take a few attempts to get the bow at the right draw strength. Once the loose knot is slid into the notch, wrap the string several times and tie it in place.

HOW TO SHOOT THE BOW

1. It's important to set some safety expectations before shooting a bow. We create a "range" in the back of the shop by taping out a safe space with a target at one end. Our little archers are only allowed to shoot their bows when an adult is present, and they must stand at the end of the field with no one else in front of them. An arrow should never be pointed at another person or animal.

2. To shoot the bow, insert the bowstring into the nock. Holding the bow so the arrow rests on the hand holding the bow, use 2 fingers like bunny ears to pinch and hold the arrow at the nock. Pull the bowstring back just enough to create tension on the bowstring. Pull the bow up. Aim at the target and release the bunny ears. This takes practice! Fumbling is part of the process.

Guiding Questions

- How do you feel about hunting?
- How can a bow and arrow be used for play or sport (without hurting anyone)?
- Why is it important to understand how our ancestors got food?
- How can we be safe?
- What expectations do we need to set about this new toy?
- Some cultures use archery as a form of meditation. Why do you think that is?

Extensions

FOR EVERYONE

- Sew a quiver for your arrows using scrap fabric.
- Research different bow designs from around the world.
- Make your own target with a cardboard box.

FOR KIDS AGES 4 AND UNDER / DELAYED MOTOR SKILLS

- Caregiver creates and little one decorates.

FOR KIDS AGES 8 AND UP / ADVANCED MOTOR AND CREATIVE SKILLS

- Consider attaching real arrowheads.
- Experiment with lashing techniques for the feathers.

FIVE

MAKING HERBAL SALVES

This simple project has been a staple at the shop since we opened, and I often hear from kids that they love creating something that feels healing and helpful. Also, kids love good smells and melting stuff! The results of this project are elevated even more when the ingredients are foraged from plants in your community. My kids carry their homemade salves to use as lip balm or a bug-bite cure, and to soothe those pesky hot-glue burns.

Every summer we take groups of kids into the neighborhood around our shop, which is located in a community just east of downtown Denver, to explore the natural world. Many of our kids are lifelong city kids who don't have a ton of experience interacting with nature. If they do, often they have never slowed down long enough to notice all of the things happening right in their own backyards and playgrounds. We walk the one mile each day to City Park, a sprawling turn-of-the-century urban park. The first day we walk, I ask the kids to quietly notice the world around them. What plants do they see? The trees? The insects? The animals? How does the sun shine on the sidewalk?

Anywhere we are, nature is working to make itself known. Plants and insects are in our spaces—even if it's a dandelion poking up through the cracks in the sidewalk. We've learned to ignore the natural environment around us in so many ways. What if we slowed down enough to just notice what's going on? Just like the sit spot, the act of noticing can be profound for children. It's as if all of the things they've never seen come clearly into view.

By teaching kids to be observers, we teach them to slow down, to analyze, and to ask questions. Before I started this work, I could barely identify one-tenth of the trees in our community, and I could scarcely name a plant. There are tons of great regional plant and animal guides both in print and online. I highly recommend buying paper copies for your little explorers to keep in their backpacks.

5-Ways Challenge

We can use simple themes or questions to focus the work of children. In the inspiring world of Reggio Emilia, these are known as provocations. The Reggio Emilia approach is an educational philosophy founded in the post–WWII era. The foundational principals include self-directed and experiential learning for preschool and primary-aged children. Provocations are really anything that inspires thought, interest, deeper inquiry, or action. Here's a simple provocation to help your kiddos develop their knowledge of the natural world:

1. Identify 5 tree types.
2. Identify 5 types of birds.
3. Identify 5 edible or medicinal plants growing in your community.
4. Identify 5 wild animals living in your community.
5. Identify 5 insects.

Foraging Best Practices

Foraging is the practice of harvesting food and medicinal plants from the natural environment. There are a few practices that will help make foraging safe and sustainable. First and foremost, we must forage in a legal and ethical way. Check with your local and governmental agencies and always ask for permission before you harvest from private or public land. Make sure that you're 100 percent sure of the plant identity before you harvest anything. Field guides and experts are your best resources. Only harvest from clean areas. Do not harvest from roadsides, along sidewalks, or in industrial areas. It's recommended that you only harvest between one-tenth and one-third of any available plant material. This will enable the plants to continue to propagate and thrive. A good forager leaves no trace. With a little extra thought, care, and planning, foraging practices can bring us and our children closer to our natural world and provide us with thoughtful and intentional time outdoors.

MAKING HERBAL SALVES

Creating an herbal salve requires just a few relatively inexpensive ingredients and a bit of time to explore your neighborhood and watch a pot. Salves also make a great gift. There are a few plant materials that are our go-tos for salves. If they're not available or growing in your area, your natural food stores may have dried versions.

Who's It For?

- Everyone

Time Commitment

- 1 hour up to several days

Mess Level

- Waxy

What You Need

- Plant material (yarrow, lavender, sage, or chamomile; see Tip below)

- Avocado oil or olive oil

- Cheesecloth

- Double boiler or old slow cooker (find supplies at a local thrift store)

- Beeswax pellets

- Spoon

- Metal salve tins (1- to 3-ounce sizes are best) or small glass jars

OPTIONAL

- Lavender essential oil
- Airtight dark glass container

TIP: Use a large handful of plant material per cup of oil. The more plant material you use, the more potent your tincture will be. Use the whole plant if you like. The flowers, stems, and leaves of the plants all have medicinal properties; however, leaves and stems may turn your salve green.

LAVENDER

Believed to have anti-inflammatory properties that will help with bug bites and minor burns. The scent is also believed to be calming, helping reduce anxiety and aiding in sleep.

YARROW

Once used as a poultice (plant material applied to a wound to promote healing), yarrow is also believed to have antimicrobial and anti-inflammatory properties.

SAGE

Also an anti-inflammatory, sage is thought to contain antioxidants that keep skin looking young.

CHAMOMILE

Similar to yarrow, sage, and lavender, chamomile is soothing to the skin. It also may contain antifungal properties.

MAKE IT THE LONG WAY

1. Using at least 1 large handful of plant material per cup of oil, soak plant materials in an airtight container of oil for up to 2 weeks before creating the salve. Dark glass and a cool place will reduce the likelihood of spoilage.

2. Strain the infused oil using cheesecloth. You can then use the oil to create a salve (following the instructions for Make It the Short Way, below) or as you would an essential oil (perfume, candles, etc.).

MAKE IT THE SHORT WAY

1. Add plant material to a double boiler or slow cooker. Add 1 part beeswax pellets to 4 parts oil. Use your infused oil here or plain oil and heat on low for at least 1 hour. Hot wax is no joke. Have kiddos wear gloves and safety glasses. Adults should do the pouring.

2. Stir and strain using the cheesecloth.

3. Pour into salve tins or jars and allow to cool. While we wait for our salve to cool, we often create sticker labels that include an ingredient list and the potential benefits of the plant infusions. Encourage your maker to come up with a catchy brand name and logo for their new line of spa products.

Guiding Questions

➤ What does this plant do?

➤ How do we know?

➤ What happens when we melt things?

➤ How can we use plants to stay healthy?

➤ Why is it important to know about plants and animals in our community?

➤ How does it make you feel to create something that helps people feel healthy?

Extensions

EVERYONE

➤ Use your infused oils to make a sugar scrub using 1 part oil and 3 parts raw sugar.

➤ Visit your local botanical gardens to deepen your understanding of plants.

➤ Plant a foraging garden. Search for medicinal and food-providing plants that are native to your environment. Even in our small urban yard, we've planted yarrow, coneflower, lavender, sage, strawberries, raspberries, and serviceberries. Our kids love to go outside to forage for goodies. There's nothing much sweeter than watching a child eat a strawberry they've grown themselves!

FOR KIDS AGES 4 AND UNDER / DELAYED MOTOR SKILLS

➤ Practice cutting and tearing plant material.

FOR KIDS AGES 8 AND UP / ADVANCED MOTOR AND CREATIVE SKILLS

➤ Create a field journal (page 92) to collect and document plant samples using observational drawing.

➤ Use your field journal to illustrate and collect information about foraged plant materials.

PART TWO

FIBER ARTS

The world of fiber arts encompasses a wide range of skills, products, materials, and processes. In this section I will focus our attention on handwork. Handwork is fiber arts that doesn't require a sewing machine, although they're awful fun! We will explore a variety of processes and techniques that can be modified for little hands or combined in various ways with impressive results. You will find a brief history of weaving as well as conversations about community, and the balancing act of helping kids become self-sufficient, how we learn from our elders and one another, and how we observe and document our learning process.

Fiber arts help children develop fine motor skills as well as planning and process skills. They also require time, careful attention, and effort. Through work in the fiber arts, we can help children connect to historical traditions that have been passed down through the careful tutelage of our elders. There's also ample room for creative play in fiber-based crafts.

Handwork has a deep tradition in the Waldorf world and beyond, and for good reason. The Waldorf philosophy was founded nearly one hundred years ago by Rudolf Steiner. Waldorf educators place a good deal of emphasis on handwork and practical craft as a means for children to develop their creativity and self-reliance. Fiber crafts encourage detailed process work that requires children to focus deeply and quietly on the task at hand. Fiber work, like weaving and sewing, can be taken up at any moment and requires just a few key supplies. The materials needed to get started are inexpensive or often free. Children can grow their skill base over time. For very young hands, consider starting by stitching yarn onto burlap with a large plastic needle. With some dedicated practice and support, children will quickly acquire skills that will enable them to become more self-sufficient and to care for their things. What could be better?

SIX

WEAVING

Weaving has a special place in my heart. My first year of teaching, my mom's friend gifted me a rag rug that she had woven on a hundred-year-old loom on her farm. I used that rug as a primary source in my classroom. With a shoestring budget, I developed a weaving project for my students that wouldn't require buying tons of yarn.

Connecting to Our Past and Our Community

The history of textiles and fibers is of particular interest to me as a woman. Traditionally, the creation of textiles was women's work. The advent of woven textiles is difficult to date due to the ephemeral nature of textiles. The earliest evidence dates back to 5000 B.C.E. With the advent of the weaving loom, women were able to start and stop their work as childcare tasks demanded. However, the work was so laborious that little time was left for innovation, and textile weaving techniques largely did not automate until the Industrial Revolution. The creation of clothing and bedding in cultures all over the world was a primary task in everyday life. Weaving and sewing often happened in community.

I often find myself asking how I can help my own children and students connect to and understand the past. Knowing our history is important. It helps us better understand ourselves and have reverence for the way people worked and lived. One of the best and most effective ways for children to connect to our past is through spending time with elders. My children spend a great deal of time with my grandparents and parents. My grandmother was raised in a tiny mountain town outside of Boulder, Colorado. I was always fascinated by her stories of growing up during the Great Depression. She loves to tell stories about her grandmother, who raised her, and how they made do, how they helped feed their neighbors who were struggling harder than they were, how she and her sisters all shared an apartment and one job at the local five-and-dime. I still love to hear stories about what childhood was like for her and others. How they learned, played, and helped their families. My kids love it, too. They hear themselves in the stories and see themselves in old photos of my grandparents and their siblings. Through the gift of time and proximity, my children have had the opportunity to hear firsthand accounts of what childhood was like in the 1930s and 1950s. They know what kind of work was expected of children their age back then, and they're affected by the differences and similarities. Milo and Wyatt love to pore over old photos and treasure boxes and imagine what life was like for our family when they were children.

In my classroom I invited in community members to share their experiences and skills with my students. There are many ways we can encourage our children to engage with people of older generations—volunteer, participate in library programs, mow the neighbor's lawn in exchange for a cup of tea. Whatever and however you find connections, I highly encourage you to do it. Your children will be better for it.

Learning to weave can be challenging for little hands. By using upcycled fabric strips, the weaving process is simplified. The strips are easier to weave than yarn, and the process goes a bit faster. By using discarded textiles, such as old bedsheets and outgrown clothes, makers are able to create work that holds special memories while saving those items from the landfill.

Who's it for?
➤ Best for kids ages 6+

Time Commitment
➤ 2 to 8 hours

Mess Level
➤ Fabric bits

What You Need

FOR THE CARDBOARD LOOM
➤ Ruler or measuring tape
➤ Sturdy cardboard, anywhere from 4 x 6 inches to 12 x 18 inches
➤ Scissors
➤ Cotton string (for the warp)

FOR THE WEAVING
➤ Bedsheets, cotton clothing, other discarded textiles (see Tip)
➤ Large plastic needle or notched popsicle stick

OPTIONAL
➤ Yarn
➤ 6- to 8-inch stick for hanging

TIP: Prepare the fabric by cutting a 1-inch notch at the top of the fabric and then tearing it into strips. This is half the fun! For stretch fabric, such as T-shirts, cut the entire strip, as it won't tear easily.

MAKE THE LOOM

1. Using a ruler, make marks every ½ inch along the top and bottom edge of the cardboard. At each mark, make a line that is ½-inch long. Cut along the line with scissors to make notches. (See illustration.)

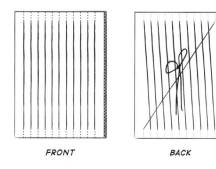

FRONT   BACK

2. Using sturdy cotton string, warp the loom by wrapping the string through each notch and around the back of the loom. Pull string tight and knot it in the back. (See illustration.)

MAKE THE WEAVING

1. Select a piece of fiber to weave with and thread the end through the needle. Try different methods for weaving.

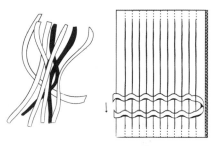

PLAIN WEAVE: Plain weave is the most basic over-under weaving pattern and snakes like an S through the warp. (See illustration.)

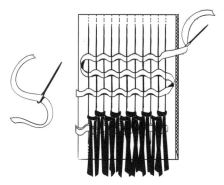

RYA (FRINGE): Rya can be used to create fringe at the bottom of a weaving or a shag-carpet effect in the body of the weaving. Cut pieces of material at least 4 inches long. Fold a piece in half and lay the center of the material over 2 warp strings. Wrap the ends over and around the warp through the middle of the 2 strings. It should look like bunny ears. Pull the material down and move 1 string over to create your next rya. Weave 1 row of plain weave between a row of rya to secure the material. (See illustration.)

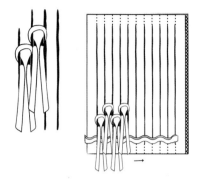

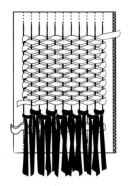

BRAIDING: This is a more advanced weaving technique. Weave material over the warp string and around, creating a loop around each warp.

3. Continue weaving using whatever combination of plain weave and rya that you like. Remember to push the row down as you go so they are tight. Once you have woven to the top of the loom, you are ready to remove the piece from the loom and finish it as a rug or a wall hanging.

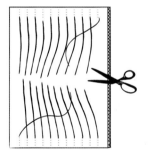

BACK

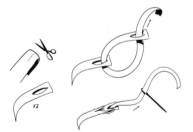

2. Add length to your cloth by snipping a hole in the working end (hole 1) and in one end of the length you are attaching (hole 2). Feed new length through hole 1, then feed the tail of new length through hole 2 and pull tight. This will attach the two pieces together without a bulky knot.

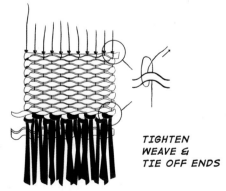

TIGHTEN WEAVE & TIE OFF ENDS

4. Once your weaving is complete, turn the loom over and snip the warp strings across the center. Carefully pull the strings away from the notches at the top and bottom of the loom. Tie 2 warp strings together at a time, securing the weaving. Repeat on the top and bottom of your weaving. Trim the warp strings, if desired.

5. Use as a doll rug or attach to a stick slightly longer than the width of the weaving by stitching around the stick and the top of the weaving with a strip of fabric. Attach another strip as a hanger to create a wall hanging.

TIGHTEN WEAVE

TIE & TRIM LOSE EDGES

TIE OFF AROUND DOWEL & TRIM

WRAP AROUND DOWEL & HANG!

Guiding Questions

➤ What is the purpose of weaving?

➤ How can we reuse materials to create something new and useful?

➤ How do patterns help us create?

➤ Why do we do things that take a long time to finish?

➤ How can we show perseverance when working on time-consuming projects?

➤ How do you feel when you do a slow craft?

Extensions

FOR EVERYONE

➤ Try weaving with a variety of materials, such as cordage, sticks, yarn, and ribbon.

➤ Make a larger loom. There are tons of great resources and loom designs online.

FOR KIDS AGES 4 AND UNDER / DELAYED MOTOR SKILLS

➤ Spread the warp string out to 1-inch spacing.

➤ Create a shuttle by cutting notches in a large popsicle stick. Wrap your fabric lengths around the shuttle and weave through.

➤ Start with paper weaving. Cut 1-inch strips in a piece of construction paper, leaving the top 1-inch portion attached. Weave alternating-color 1-inch paper strips. This is a great way for little hands to practice the over-under weaving pattern.

FOR KIDS AGES 8 AND UP / ADVANCED MOTOR AND CREATIVE SKILLS

➤ Research more advanced weaving techniques and patterns. Based on your findings, create a more intricate design.

➤ Try using the rya technique to weave the entire piece. Give it a haircut at the end to create a pile rug.

➤ Make a larger cardboard loom and work a bigger rug.

SEVEN

CREATING CORDAGE

Cordage, better known as rope, is a foundational material. Take a moment to think of all the ways a piece of string or rope could help you in a survival situation. Creating cordage from natural materials is a practice that helps kids see themselves as self-sufficient.

What does it mean to be self-sufficient? In the previous section on heritage skills, I talked about the ways in which we connect to our shared past, to our community, and to nature. While humans are inherently communal people, it's important for children to see themselves as capable of caring for themselves independently. In our Ancestral Skills camp, kids often come with romantic notions of being alone and lost in the woods, like in the book *Hatchet* (a fan favorite at our house, for sure). We talk about what it would be like if you suddenly found yourself alone in the woods. Knowing how to make a shelter and build a fire become important skills. Knowing how to create cordage or rope is also an important skill. It enables the lone person to create a fishing line and nets, to lash together tree branches, to create clothing, and so much more. However, self-sufficiency is more than just a set of specific skills. It's a mind-set, and one that too often we delay in children. We offer help when it's not needed. We remove struggle from children's lives. I think of being self-sufficient as having a set of beliefs that includes statements such as "I am capable of solving big problems" and "I can use my unique mind and capable hands to create the things I need both physically and mentally."

We can help cultivate self-sufficiency by posing problems and encouraging problem-solving. We can model this process by setting up scenarios and activities that task kids to solve problems with limited resources. Of course, this is sometimes easier said than done, and sometimes I don't take my own best advice. One morning when my oldest was eight years old, I found myself in an all-too-familiar situation. We were frantically trying to get out the door for school and work. I had asked Milo no less than a thousand times to put on his shoes, and there he was with one shoe sort of on, laces untied, and he begged for me to tie his shoes. In exasperation I bent over, tied up his laces, and said for the one-thousandth time, "Next time you have to do it yourself!"

It's hard to watch kids struggle, especially when they're our own. I have to remind myself that it's my goal as a parent and an educator to help young people develop into adults who can care for themselves. On day 1,001, I stopped tying Milo's shoes. Guess what? He could do it. He already knew how. He just needed to struggle a little bit longer to get the hang of it. We don't need to do things for children that they can do for themselves. We just need to provide the container for them to be successful.

Tips for Helping Children Be More Self-Sufficient

Here's a little cheat sheet to help you know when to let a child grapple with a challenging task.

- Do they have all of the skills (background knowledge, physical and psychological development, etc.) necessary to complete the task?

- Are they or you hungry or tired? Best to meet those primal needs before doing hard things.

- Do you or they have time to struggle or grapple with this new skill?

- Clearly state the desired task. I sometimes think children can read my mind, but they can't.

- Start small. Small successes lead to bigger ones. Ask your child to put their cup in the sink after lunch, and the next thing you know, they're loading the dishwasher just the way you like!

- Remind yourself that it's okay if it's not perfect. No one does things perfect when they're learning.

- Look for the successes. Remember that praise and encouragement go a lot further than harsh critique.

CREATING CORDAGE

Creating cordage is a wonderful act of self-sufficiency. If you have the woods to harvest from, it's even more of a thrill for a child to learn a skill that could potentially save their own life in an emergency. Making cordage, much like tying shoes, takes a bit of practice and fine motor skills, but once mastered, it's easy to pick up and play.

Who's It For?

- Best for kids ages 6+

Time Commitment

- 30 minutes to 3 hours

Mess Level

- Bits of loose material.

What You Need

- 2 yards plant fibers (see Tip)
- Tape

TIP: *There are a variety of plant materials that are just right for creating cordage, including the inner bark of many trees such as cottonwood, aspen, juniper, and elm. Tall grasses and yucca also make good plant fibers. Look for long-stranded material that can be made pliable by tearing the plant down the center. In a pinch, natural raffia makes great cordage (available at craft/dollar stores).*

over strand A. Then turn both strands one half turn clockwise. Repeat this pattern. (See illustration.)

1. Grab at least 2 strands of whatever material you've selected.

2. Tape the ends to a surface, then twist the material together clockwise until it binds over on itself in the middle of the length of strands. There's a 2-step process to the twist that can feel a little tricky. Holding strand A in your hand, twist it one half turn clockwise, then place the twisted strand over strand B and twist both strands one half turn clockwise. Then grab strand B, twist one half turn clockwise, and place

3. Add material as needed by twisting a new strand onto each end and repeating the A-B pattern.

Guiding Questions

➤ Why should we do the hard things?

➤ What are all the ways you can use cordage?

➤ Why is this an important survival skill?

➤ How does this process create strong cordage?

➤ What could you do to make your work stronger?

Extensions

FOR EVERYONE

➤ Build a shelter using the cordage you've created to lash your structure together.

➤ Lash together sticks by weaving your cordage around a set of them to create a toy boat. Set sail!

➤ Incorporate your cordage into a weaving or sewing project.

FOR KIDS AGES 4 AND UNDER / DELAYED MOTOR SKILLS

➤ Twisting is a great fine motor skill. Tie yarn or raffia to a nail in a board or simply tape it to a table. Practice twisting.

FOR KIDS AGES 8 AND UP / ADVANCED MOTOR AND CREATIVE SKILLS

➤ Research the available plant material in your community.

➤ Gather (always with permission) and test out a variety of materials to determine the best cordage material available. Document your findings in your field journal (page 92).

➤ Create a length challenge. Make at least 6 continuous feet of consistent and strong cordage.

EIGHT

MENDING

Mending and patching clothing with kids is a great way for them to actively participate in caring for their things. These skills also allow kids to personalize their clothes in unique ways. We have a drop-in time at the shop called "Mending Mondays," when anyone can come by with their pile of mending. We provide needles, thread, fusible interfacing (great for reinforcing knees), and darning eggs. We talk, we mend, we feel proud that we've taken the time to care for our things. Kids as young as four will help stitch their worn knees back together using visible mending. Visible mending is the practice of adding stitches to a garment that are intentionally visible.

Make Do and Mend

The phrase *make do and mend* was coined during World War II when textiles and other materials were funneled into the war effort, making them scarce for the civilian population. "Make Do and Mend" was a wartime effort issued by the British Ministry of Information meant to encourage housewives to be both frugal and stylish in the midst of this tumultuous era. During this time, textiles were in short supply as raw materials and commercial factories were used to create textiles for uniforms, army blankets, and more. Women were expected to mend their clothing, make new clothing out of what they could upcycle from their attic, and embrace this DIY mentality as a style to be desired. We all could use a bit more of the "Make Do and Mend" attitude, for the planet and for our own well-being.

We live in a culture that puts a high value on newness. So often we want our clothing to be perfect, new and fresh. However, there's a growing slow fashion and conservation movement that takes its cues from the past. Mending clothing has become an art form. The results are beautiful, and the practice allows us to bring thoughtful attention to the care of our clothing. What better way to get kids involved with starting to conserve resources than to combine ecology with a little fashion!

I have two high-energy kids, and they go through pants like nobody's business. We went the route of inexpensive fast-fashion, throwaway clothes, but I was really feeling the impact of creating waste. Textile waste is a huge environmental problem. I wanted my boys to start environmentally friendly wardrobe practices now—meaning, I want them to feel the love of thrift; to have an attitude that less is more, quality beats quantity every day, and just because they've lost a button or torn a knee doesn't mean that they can't mend what's been broken.

A blown-out knee may be the most common mending fix needed, if your kids are anything like mine. Mending and patching a torn knee is a great way to stretch the life of a pair of pants. Your kids can also add personal touches to their wardrobes by using their favorite colors and bright fabric patches.

Who's It For?

➤ Best for kids ages 6+

Time Commitment

➤ 10 minutes to hours

Mess Level

➤ Bits of string

What You Need

➤ Scrap fabric

➤ Double-sided fusible interfacing

➤ Scissors

➤ Iron

➤ Thread

➤ No. 18 embroidery needle

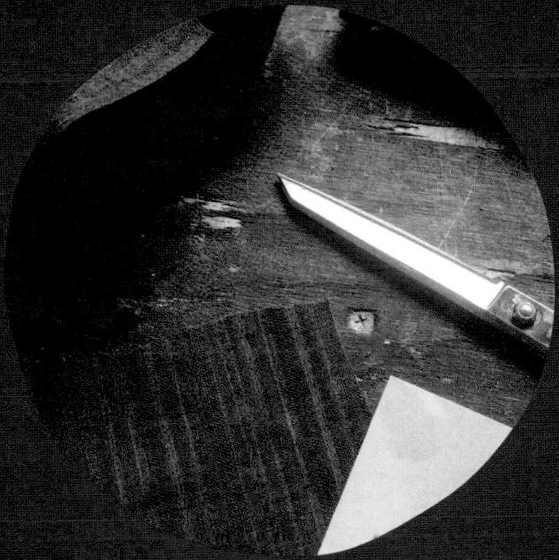

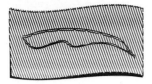

1. To make an internal patch, cut a piece of scrap fabric and a piece of double-sided fusible interfacing roughly a ½ inch bigger all around than the hole to be patched. Leave the protective sheet on for now.

2. Cut a hole in the interfacing the same size as the hole to be patched, so it doesn't show through when the patch is in place. Iron the interfacing onto the front side of the fabric patch.

3. Align the patch on the inside of the hole to be mended and peel the protective sheet from the interfacing. Iron to fuse the patch to the pant leg. Now you have a strong patch to stitch around.

4. Use the needle and thread to stitch around the patch, securing it in place. I like to take a free-form approach to mending with kids. A simple running or whipstitch back

and forth around the patch will look lovely and add strength to the patch. This is great practice for any hand-sewing or free-form embroidery.

TIP: *Threading a needle: Cut a length of thread that goes hand to hand with your arms spread like an eagle (a wingspan). Push the end of the thread through the hole of a no. 18 sharp embroidery needle—these have a nice wide eye and are easy to thread for most kids ages 6 and up. This is best achieved if the end of the thread is smooth. When I learned to thread a needle, I was taught to leave a 6-inch tail and tie endless knots at the end and hope it doesn't pull through. There's a better way! For kids, we double over the thread, make the first stitch, then tie the tail and the running thread in a square knot at the back. If your child can tie their shoes, they can make a square knot. This is a much more secure attachment and will ensure that the thread isn't unthreaded with each stitch.*

CHAIN STITCH

CROSS STITCH

Guiding Questions

➦ Why would we mend this item?

➦ Why not just throw these away?

➦ How are our clothes made?

➦ How does it affect the environment?

➦ How can we express our personality and values without clothes?

Extensions

FOR EVERYONE

➦ Create iron-on patches using cloth, the double-sided fusible interfacing, and permanent markers.

➦ Mend using a variety of embroidery stitches.

➦ Sew on your patch from the outside.

FOR KIDS AGES 4 AND UNDER / DELAYED MOTOR SKILLS

➦ Have your child practice their scissor skills by cutting bits of fabric scraps.

➦ Share the work. Have your child pull the needle through and guide the needle back in.

FOR KIDS AGES 8 AND UP / ADVANCED MOTOR AND CREATIVE SKILLS

➦ Try mindful mending. Have your child practice mending their clothes as a form of meditation.

➦ Look for *sashiko* patterns and alternative approaches to mending. Sashiko is a historic mending practice from Japan dating back six hundred years. Using running stitches and patterned stitches, worn garments are reinforced with visible mending patterns.

➦ Have your child tend to their own mending pile every so often (especially before they ask for something new)!

NINE

HAND SEWING A STUFFIE

Learning to sew by hand used to be a sort of rite of passage. I remember pulling a shoelace through a lacing card in preschool and learning to hand sew at five, and I was known to work a few overly ambitious cross-stitch projects in my upper elementary years. Hand sewing is a skill that is best taught one on one or in a very small group. It requires the teacher to be physically close to the student in order to carefully observe the child as they begin to stitch. This requires a great deal of trust between the elder and child.

My own kids learned to sew by helping me pull the needle through a stitch on my work, threading a needle for me, or putting their thumb down on the thread while I tied a knot—all learning

through assisting their elder (me!).

Hand sewing, embroidery, and cross-stitch are slow crafts that build hand-eye coordination, problem-solving skills, and creativity.

The Craftsman and Apprentice

If you're reading this, chances are you're the elder—the person with the skills and knowledge to teach the child. How do we help children have respect and curiosity for the knowledge and skills that an older person holds? We named our shop The Craftsman & Apprentice for a reason. The craftsman is the elder—the person with the knowledge and skills to share. The apprentice is the seeker of that knowledge. Traditionally an apprentice works alongside the craftsman, helping them with everyday tasks while they observe and absorb the skills of the craftsman. What if we thought of our relationships with children in this way? Children can help with tasks as

they grow and take on more responsibility. Gradually their help and contribution lead organically to knowledge. Apprenticing is different from listening to and appreciating the experiences of our elders. It's about respecting and seeking knowledge and skills-based practices from those with more experience.

This idea extends beyond a one-on-one relationship between an elder and a child, to how we engage with our communities. Informally, social capital consists of the bonds, shared values, and trust we create within our communities. When we work with children, we're helping them build positive social capital, especially when we work one on one. Think of it as a way to create a bankable social fabric that, given positive intent, helps people exist within a safe and trusting community. When positive social capital is high in a community, individuals benefit socially and emotionally from shared knowledge, skills, and ideas. In other words, when people support each other, we all win.

SEWING A STUFFIE

We have no less than seven hundred stuffies stashed under my kids' beds. Each one has a name and a sentimental origin story. Stuffies are beloved playthings and cherished security objects for most kids. This project enables kids to learn to sew but also to create their own beloved characters.

Who's it for?

Best for kids ages 5+

Time Commitment

1 to 2 hours

Mess Level

Bits of fabric and string

What You Need

Sheet of paper

Paper scissors

Felt sheets or scrap fabric

Fabric scissors

Embroidery floss

No. 18 embroidery needle

Permanent marker

Stuffing

OPTIONAL

Straight pins

Spray glue

Buttons

Bric-a-brac

Yarn

TIP: Permanent markers—I know, scary, right? My oldest son was obsessed with permanent markers as a three-year-old. I'll admit, I can still faintly see his artistic use of the marker on the brick on our front porch. Use your own best judgment here. A little scaffolding goes a long way. It can be a real privilege for kids to use the "fancy" markers by demonstrating safe and appropriate use, only on the objects we're creating and not on the dog or your brother.

1. Using a sheet of paper, draw a big shape (for newbies, a blobby, organic shape is a great start). This will be the pattern.

2. Cut out your pattern and set it aside.

3. Choose your felt or fabric, and make sure you have enough for two sides. Layer or fold the felt wrong sides (the back sides of the pieces) together. Place the pattern on the doubled felt. You can choose to pin it, hold it, or use a touch of spray glue to tack it on temporarily.

4. Cut out the shape. No need for a seam allowance.

5. Choose your embellishments for your stuffie's face. Buttons and felt scraps make great additions. Attach your embellishments to the fabric.

SEWING A BUTTON: When sewing with kids, we've found that doubling the thread and tying it off on the end helps reduce the frustration of trying to keep a needle threaded and makes for a more durable stitch. Measure a wingspan (hand to hand with your arms outstretched like an eagle) of thread and cut. Carefully put the end of the thread through the eye of the needle and pull the thread down so the needle is halfway down the length of the thread. Pair up the ends of the thread and make an overhand knot at the bottom.

From the back side of the front piece, push the needle through to the front of the front. Put the needle through the button from the back to the front. Place the needle through the next button hole and through the front of the fabric to the back. Pull through. Repeat with additional button holes or buttons. No need to change thread each time, just move the position of the thread from the back side and begin to sew another button on. To finish, tie a knot at the back.

APPLIQUÉ: To sew on or appliqué fabric eyes or other parts, simply begin at the back as you did with the button, this time pushing the needle up through the first layer and the piece you wish to attach. Using small stitches, sew up and down, being mindful to pull the needle through completely after each stitch.

6. Once all the embellishments are attached, it's time to sew your stuffie together. For first-time sewers, I recommend using a permanent marker to create a dot pattern around the edge of the stuffie to act as a stitch guide. Thread a needle using two wingspans worth of embroidery floss. Begin to stitch the front and back of the stuffie together using a whipstitch. (See illustration.) This just means placing the needle in the same side each time. Basically, poke through the dot and pull the thread through. Continue stitching around the stuffie until about 3 inches of space is left. Insert stuffing until full. Stitch the opening shut and tie the end of the thread to secure.

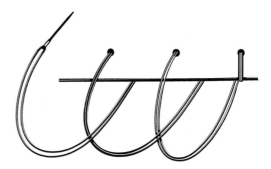

Guiding Questions

→ Why is it important to know how to sew?

→ How were clothes and toys made before machines?

→ How can we design a toy with personality?

→ How do the materials and colors that we choose make us feel?

Extensions

FOR EVERYONE

→ Make a double-sided stuffie with two moods, such as a happy face on one side and a mad face on the other side.

FOR KIDS AGES 4 AND UNDER / DELAYED MOTOR SKILLS

→ We always begin kids sewing with burlap, an embroidery hoop, a plastic needle, and yarn. The open weave of the burlap is easy for little hands to push through, and the large needle and yarn are just right for preschool hands.

FOR KIDS AGES 8 AND UP / ADVANCED MOTOR AND CREATIVE SKILLS

→ Consider making your stuffie in parts and pieces. Arms, legs, and head can all be created separately and stitched together. Grab your favorite snuggly and examine how it's made. Where are the seams? Can you reverse engineer it?

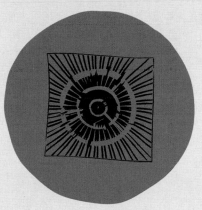

TEN

NATURAL DYES

In recent years, plant dying has become a popular craft, and for good reason: it connects us to our past and to the earth. Playing with natural dyes is one of my favorite things to do with children. It's like a potions class. We experiment, make a hypothesis, take notes, observe, and reflect. The scientific process never looked so good. Before there were chemical dyes, plant and other natural materials were used to dye textiles. From elderberries to lichen, nature is full of color. We can use natural dyes as a way of opening children's eyes to the colors of the earth.

It's important to stay playful when experimenting with natural-dye processes, and we as caregivers can model curiosity rather than striving for perfect products. There are so many factors that can affect the outcome of a dye vat. Materials, time, temperature, mordant, and

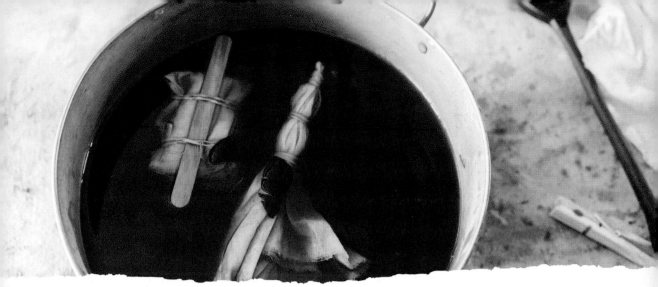

fabric composition can all change the outcomes of your dyes. A mordant is anything that helps fix the dye to the fabric. Alum, better known as cream of tartar, is often used as a simple fixative as well as a color brightener. Mordants are typically acid or alkali, and the mordant you use will depend on the pH of the dye itself. There's also a wealth of information (often conflicting) about natural dyes on the web.

Field Journals

My husband has a bit of an obsession with field journals and notebooks, and both my children have caught the bug—so much so that I invested in a vintage saddle-style binding stapler just to offset the cost of their store-bought journals. We can now crank out three-staple field journals for pennies!

In the "Heritage Skills" section, I wrote briefly about observing the world. Observation, reflection, and record keeping are all part of the creative process. As an

artist, I kept copious notes and sketchbooks. I documented everything, from all of my thoughts in a day (so many thoughts!) to glaze recipes and firing results. We often begin our work with kids by creating small notebooks specific to the work at hand. This natural-dye project is a great example of how we can weave documentation and reflection into a fun and creative experience.

Try making small paper notebooks and having your children record their observations, ideas, and thoughts. Even kiddos who aren't writing quite yet love to draw pictures to represent their experiences. Here are a few sentence stems to help get things started:

I wonder _____ .

I see _____ .

I notice _____ .

I am most proud of _____ because _____ .

My biggest challenge was _____ because _____ .

My super skills are _____ .

We'll be making a natural dye that works best with plant fibers, such as cotton. Protein fibers, such as wool, often require different dye processes. Use your new textiles for a variety of projects, including patches, hand-sewn items, or even prayer-style flags. Try dyeing any 100 percent cotton material, including T-shirts, grocery bags, and bedsheets.

Who's It For?

➡ Best for kids ages 5+

Time Commitment

➡ 90 minutes to 2 hours

Mess Level

➡ Stainy and wet

What You Need

➡ 100 percent cotton fabric

➡ Dish soap

➡ Rubber bands or string

➡ Water

➡ A dedicated nonreactive pot (thrift store!)

➡ Pits and skins from 5 to 6 avocados (see Tip)

➡ Wooden spoon

TIP: *The composition of the metals in your pots and spoons can affect the results of a dye bath. A wooden spoon and a stainless steel or enamel pot are best.*

TIP: *Carefully wash and dry the avocado pits and skins over the course of several weeks or, as in our house, one epic day of avocado toast. Freeze your collection as you go. The pits and skins tend to make brighter dyes when frozen rather than when allowed to dry. The more pits and skins you use, the darker your dye will be.*

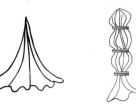

PULL

BAND

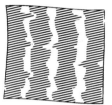

FOLD

BAND

1. Scour the fabric by washing it with dish soap. This will help remove the sizing and expose the fibers. You will want to start the dye process with a damp cloth. If you allow your scoured fabric to dry, soak it briefly before adding it to the dye pot.

2. Tie rubber bands or string tightly around your cotton fabric to create tie-dye patterns, if desired. (See illustration.)

3. Prepare the dye vat: Measure out enough water to cover your fabric and allow it to move freely in the pot. Add the water to your dye vat. Add the avocado pits and skins to the water.

4. Heat your dye vat to steaming. A low simmer seems to bring out the color best and is safer when working with little hands. After about 30 minutes, add your fabric to the dye vat.

5. Using a wooden spoon, stir the fabric. Check the fabric every 10 to 15 minutes to observe color changes. Once you've reached your desired color, remove the fabric from the dye bath. Carefully squeeze out the dye water, then hang the fabric to dry. Once dry, rinse the fabric with warm/cool water. To get the deepest shades possible, remove the dye vat from heat and allow the fabric to soak overnight in the dye bath.

Guiding Questions

➼ What are some factors that affect the color of the dye?

➼ How did people discover and perfect plant-based dyes?

➼ What are some other things that would make good dyes?

Extensions

FOR EVERYONE

➼ Experiment with plants from your garden or community; or with colorful food scraps, such as beets, onion skins, and turmeric.

➼ Try dying wood pieces, hard-boiled eggs, wool, and other fibers.

FOR KIDS AGES 4 AND UNDER / DELAYED MOTOR SKILLS

➼ All kids can help stir, cut fabric, and do some careful observations.

FOR KIDS AGES 8 AND UP / ADVANCED MOTOR AND CREATIVE SKILLS

➼ Create a dye journal and include fabric samples along with dyer notes, such as water temperature, time, dyestuff, mordants, and more. The more information you document, the better able you will be to recreate successful dye processes and avoid the ones that don't work well.

PART THREE

WOOD-WORKING

We do two things at the shop: we build real skills and we develop creative practices. Woodworking often falls squarely in the real skills category. Woodworking can be all about following plans, precision, safety, and process. I find the practices of woodworking a refreshing balance to some of the more open, creative work-play that we do. There's an end goal in mind, often a practical one. There's a purpose to the project and structure to the process. However, woodworking with children can be a creative practice as well. Creativity requires process, after all. I learned that in order to break the rules, we must know the rules. When we develop a depth of knowledge, we can then draw upon that knowledge base to experiment, break rules, and innovate. Woodworking allows children to be problem-solvers, to follow plans, and to learn to use tools safely to get desired results. Not to mention it's just plain fun to get messy, use tools, and make something real.

There's not much more satisfying than creating a useful object. It's in our nature to create for a purpose. When a child builds an object of use and function, they have had an experience of concrete creation. They have added value to the world in a very real way. This practice of practical contribution is no less valuable than creative and artistic endeavors. We often discount or dismiss these practices in our culture. However, just as we find satisfaction in cooking and cleaning, the practical skill of woodworking can bring great joy to a child. Again, there's an inherent psychological value in learning and trusting our ability to build something with our hands.

This section is all about process. We will explore how we prepare to work, why we do the work we do, and how traditions shift and shape us. I believe that making for the sake of making is in and of itself important. However, we can put our hands to good use, creating things that help the world be a little better, one bee hotel or workbench at a time.

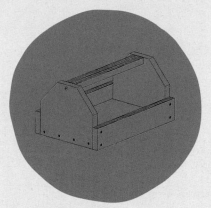

ELEVEN

TOOLBOX

My sculpture professor in college always said, "Right tool, right job." In woodworking, this couldn't be truer. In order to really do woodworking with kids, a few essential tools and skills are required. Start small and acquire new tools as needed and as space allows. It takes time to build a proper shop, and you may find that you're not doing woodworking projects often enough to warrant the investment. A small toolbox with the essentials is all you really need to get started.

Building Community through Tools

If you live in or near a city, chances are there's a tool library or community woodshop in your area. Many local public libraries have also begun tool checkouts. These places are fantastic. You can check out tools as needed, pop in to use the community woodshop, or take a class to build your skills. I would also recommend reaching out to neighbors to borrow tools. A kind favor in return is often all that is required.

Here in Denver, there's a little shop in the heart of downtown called Charlie's Second Hand Tools (we call it Second Hand Charlie's). It has been in the same location and run by the same family since the 1920s. It's a magical place filled to the brim with used tools. Whenever we walk through the doors, Steve, the owner, is ready to greet us with a smile and a sweet treat for the kids. Once, when the kids were young, we

went on our Saturday visit to the shop. We hadn't stopped by in a while, and Steve and the other shop manager, Steve (yes, Steve and Steve), seemed extra-excited to see us. They had a surprise for the boys. Steve and Steve had used old scrap wood to make the kids a mini workbench outfitted with a sweet vintage vice. All of the project photos in this book are shot on that little workbench, and it now has a prized location in the shop. I was struck that our community friends would take the time to use their skills and resources to make something so special for our kids. Community is so important. Doing for others and going out of your way to create special and thoughtful experiences for children helps build their trust and optimism. They, in turn, may become the adults who create special experiences for children. What can you and your children do with your unique skills and talents to give back to your community or make someone's day?

GETTING STARTED IN WOODWORKING

How you begin using tools and woodworking with kids will depend greatly on the space and resources you have available. In the following section, I break down my favorite and most useful tools as well as simple ways to begin to develop a safe and functional space for woodworking.

GATHERING TOOLS

Below is a list of hand and power tools that make a great start to a woodshop—I've listed them in order of frequency of use/cost. A word of caution: buying and acquiring tools can easily become an obsession. My husband and I often joke that our growing tool collection forced us to open the shop.

ESSENTIALS

- Safety glasses (kid-sized glasses can be found online)
- 120 grit sandpaper
- Work gloves
- Measuring tape
- Speed square
- Pencil
- Dust mask
- Ear protection
- Wood glue
- 1- to 1½-inch nails
- Screws

HAND TOOLS

- Screwdriver
- Hammer
- Pliers
- Hole saw
- Saw
- Clamps/vises

POWER TOOLS

- Drill with a variety of bits
- Miter saw
- Bandsaw
- Belt sander
- Palm sander
- Jigsaw
- Scroll saw
- Table saw
- Planer

SETTING UP A WOODWORKING AREA

Setting up a woodworking area may look a bit different from your primary maker space or it can be incorporated into your other work space. If you'd like to set up a dedicated woodworking space, here are a few tips.

Use pegboard against a wall to hang hand tools, such as screwdrivers and hammers. Organize your wood stock into categories: 2 x 4s, common board, flat boards, plywood, and scrap.

Sawdust is no good for you, and little ones are more affected by dust than many adults. Be thoughtful about how you contain dust. If you're using a power tool such as a chop saw, attach a shop vac to the back; or at the very least, empty dust bags regularly and vacuum after each use.

Have a dedicated work surface that can withstand hammering, drilling, and gluing. I've had great luck finding old workbenches on swap sites, or build your own kid-sized workbench as a collaborative project. Plans abound on the internet.

Make your space inside or out. I once created a woodworking area for a client just outside their indoor work space, under an awning. This allowed the kids to have fresh air while not having to worry about making messes indoors. Depending on the age and experience of your child, a woodworking space can be used by the whole family.

This toolbox is an inexpensive and simple first woodworking project. Once they've completed it, your little carpenter will have a special place to store their tools and supplies. Cedar is a relatively soft wood that makes nailing a breeze for little hands.

Who's It For?

Best for kids ages 5+

Time Commitment

1 to 2 hours

Mess Level

Sawdust and glue

What You Need

- Saw (miter saw preferred)
- One 6-inch x 6-foot cedar fence picket
- Speed square
- One 10-inch piece 1-inch x 2-inch pine board
- Drill with a small drill bit for pilot holes, and hex bit
- 120 grit sandpaper
- Wood glue
- Hammer
- 1-inch finish nails
- Two 1½-inch screws
- Measuring tape
- Safety glasses

OPTIONAL

- *Paint*
- *Embellishments*
- *Paintbrushes*

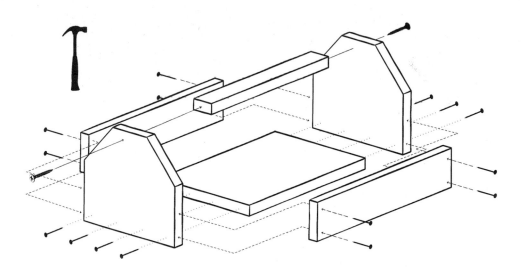

1. Using the miter saw, cut the cedar as follows:

- Cut 2 pieces for the ends: 5½ (board width) x 5 inches.

- Trim the top of both endpieces: Using a speed square, measure two 45-degree angles at the top, with 2½ inches left in the center. Cut the angles.

- Cut 1 piece for the bottom: 5½ x 11 inches. Cut 2 pieces for the sides: 2½ x 11 inches.

2. Using the miter saw, cut the pine board as follows:

- Cut 1 piece for the handle: 1½ x 10 inches.

3. Mark and drill pilot holes for the nails according to the plan. (See illustration.)

4. Sand all the pieces with the sandpaper. Sanding is a great fine motor task, and the sound is oh so sweet.

5. Starting with the long sidepieces, run a bead of glue along a long edge. Line up the pieces with the bottom, one side at a time, and hammer nails through the pilot holes. It's important to remind your little ones to line up the wood pieces exactly in order, to have the box fit together. If their first attempt is less than square, pry the nails and try again before the glue sets. It's always okay to try things again when needed.

6. Attach the endpieces using the same procedure.

7. Apply glue to the ends of the handle and center the handle piece between the two endpieces. With help, drill a pilot hole into the endpiece through to the handle on each end. Using a screw, attach the handle on each side. A screw is a more secure attachment and will last longer with the inevitable wear and tear of carrying the box by the handle.

8. Give the whole box a good finish sanding.

9. Paint, personalize, and decorate as desired.

Guiding Questions

➤ How can we be safe when working with tools and wood?

➤ Why is it important to plan ahead?

➤ How can we measure carefully and accurately?

➤ Why do we do things in steps? How would this work if we didn't have a plan?

Extensions

FOR EVERYONE

➤ Decorate and personalize your toolbox.

➤ Headphones and work gloves can be used for anyone with increased auditory and sensory needs.

FOR KIDS AGES 4 AND UNDER / DELAYED MOTOR SKILLS

➤ Have all pieces prepped and ready to assemble? A pair of pliers can be used to hold a nail in place while little hands practice hammering. Sanding is a fantastic fine motor and tactile activity.

FOR KIDS AGES 8 AND UP / ADVANCED MOTOR AND CREATIVE SKILLS

➤ Design, cut, and build your own custom toolbox.

➤ Use a wood burner to embellish and personalize your box.

➤ Cut the letters of your name from ⅛-inch plywood using a scroll saw. Attach with wood glue.

TWELVE

BEE HOTEL

Children seem to naturally be drawn to insects. Insects are curious creatures, and just watching them do their work can provide hours of entertainment. They're also excellent barometers of the health of our environment. Bee populations have been on the decline all over the world, and bees are an integral component of our food cycle.

One year when I was still teaching in public schools, I was able to spend half my time developing project-based learning opportunities for elementary-age students. I've always believed that people learn best when they're contributing something real to the world around them. We learned to worm compost. We built community gardens. We fundraised for water projects. We learned all about the plight of bees. Whenever possible, we brought in experts from our community to deepen our understanding and learn how to truly help. Being a citizen means

thinking deeply about the world around us and actively taking steps to make the world a better place. There's much work to be done to make our world a better place for all. We can use our hands and skills to contribute to that work.

Working with Kids on Big Problems

The world can feel awful scary as we face climate change and more. How do we help children become change makers without also giving them adult-level stress and anxiety? As much as I preach independence and self-reliance, I also feel it's important that children retain their inherent optimism and trust in the world. As kids grow up, they're exposed to and absorb more and more of the big world. This can mean that our children learn about the hard parts of humanity: war, famine,

discrimination, and climate change. When our kids come with big questions, we can respond with kindness, an open ear, and thoughtful responses. My mother always reassured me that there are good people in the world working to make it better and that we can be those people, too. She would answer my questioning mind by turning the questions back to me.

- What do you think?
- If you could, how would you solve the problem?
- What can you do today to help?
- How can we start here at home?

We're all capable of being agents of change—in our homes, our communities, and the world. When we work with our hands and our minds and one another, big things can happen.

BEE HOTEL

This bee hotel project is so sweet. If you're looking for a way to combine craft, activism, and science, this is the perfect project. As your kiddos build their bee hotels, they will learn a valuable lesson about helping the earth and its tiniest inhabitants. This project was codeveloped by Anna Loring.

Who's It For?
- Best for kids ages 5+

Time Commitment
- 90 minutes to 2 hours

Mess Level
- Sawdust

What You Need
- One 6-inch x 6-foot cedar fence picket
- Miter saw or handsaw
- Sandpaper
- Drill with a small bit for pilot holes
- 1-inch finish nails
- Wood glue
- Bee tubes (available online)

OPTIONAL
- Moss and pine cones
- Hot glue gun with wood glue sticks (these are so cool!!)
- Eye hook

TIP: *Let's talk about glue guns for a moment. It's no exaggeration to say that we use glue guns every day at the shop. Low-temperature hot glue guns are indispensable craft tools. Why? Making quick and mostly permanent attachments allows kids to work as fast as their imagination. Also, they're a little dangerous. A burn from a hot glue gun is no fun, but it's not catastrophic. Kids learn pretty quickly to be present and thoughtful while using hot glue. We allow kids ages five and up to use hot glue guns independently. We also offer leather gloves and silicone finger protectors.*

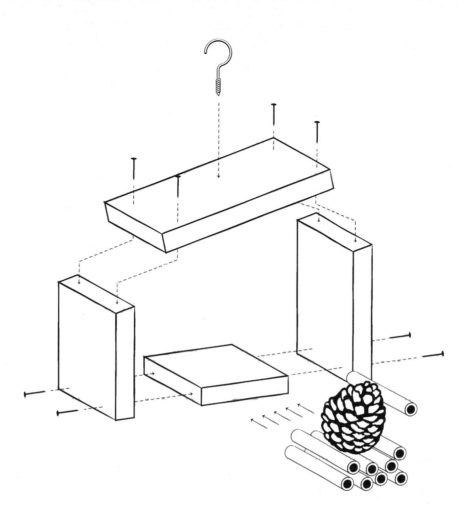

1. Cut the cedar as follows:

• Cut 1 piece for the bottom: 5½ x 3 inches.

• Cut 1 piece for right side: 5½ x 4¼ inches; cut the top edge at a 33-degree angle.

• Cut 1 piece for left side: 5½ x 3¼ inches; cut the top edge at a 33-degree angle.

• Cut 1 piece for the top: 5½ x 6 inches.

2. Sand all the pieces.

3. Mark and drill the pilot holes according to the plan. (See illustration.)

4. Glue and nail the sides to the bottom. (Don't put the roof on until the end.)

5. Begin gluing and arranging the bee tubes from the bottom to the top. This is where the hot wood glue comes in handy. Be mindful that the roof piece still needs to be attached. Add a few pieces of moss or pine cones into the mix.

6. Attach the roof using wood glue and nails.

Guiding Questions

➼ How can we help the environment?

➼ How can we help solve big problems with small actions?

➼ Why are bees an important part of the ecosystem?

Extensions

FOR EVERYONE
➼ Research bees specific to your area and the best habitats and plants for them.

FOR KIDS AGES 4 AND UNDER / DELAYED MOTOR SKILLS
➼ Grown-ups assist with construction.

FOR KIDS AGES 8 AND UP / ADVANCED MOTOR AND CREATIVE SKILLS
➼ Research and design your own bee hotel.

THIRTEEN

LIMBERJACKS

The year before we opened the shop, my brother gave me the first three *Foxfire* books. If you've never heard of them, they're compilations of how-to projects based on interviews of folks living in Appalachia in the early 1970s. The books chronicle American handcraft and folk art traditions. As you may have already surmised, I'm taken with handcraft traditions. The *Foxfire* books remind me that to know the ways of our ancestors, of our communities as they move between time and culture, is invaluable to our own approach to living. Folk art traditions are simply the ways of making within a community of people at any given time. The folk art traditions of Appalachia have been preserved in many ways due to the publication of these books. These books rekindled traditions that were popular in the 1970s during the back-to-earth movement. I see the same movement happening now. People seem to have a desire for simplicity, to make with their hands, and to do better by the world. By practicing and carrying on folk art traditions (with permission), we can connect with our collective past and find new ways into the future.

references traditional European fairy tales like "Jack and the Beanstalk" and "Jack and Jill." We can be inspired to create our own dancing, singing, and storytelling puppets.

Storytelling

I don't know about you, but I've spent a good portion of my time listening to kids tell me some serious big-fish stories. You know the kind: the story starts out with a grain of truth, such as going on a hike, and ends up with a child trying to convince you that they most definitely rode a moose through the woods. Storytelling is a wonderful way for children to connect to their world, their imagination, and our collective past. Storytelling and puppet play have also been shown to help children express big emotions.

Try using a storytelling provocation with the limberjack project. Have your kiddos imagine their limberjacks as characters in stories. These stories can and will change as they make and play. Oral storytelling changes and shifts organically, even with adults. To start, ask your children questions:

- What is your character's name?
- Are they human or animal?
- Where do they live?
- Do they have a job?
- What happens in your story?
- Are they happy, sad, excited, or all of the above?

One folk art tradition that I found in these books is the limberjack. Limberjacks combine the experiences of craft, music, and storytelling. Originating in France and popular in Appalachia, limberjacks are wooden puppets with loose joints and an attached stick that allows a puppeteer to make the puppet dance. A small wooden board is also used as a dance stage on the lap of the puppeteer. The resulting sound of the puppet striking the board as it dances sounds similar to clogging. The name "limberjack"

We've grown to love the power of puppets as a tool for creative play. This limberjack project will enable your child to create a character with which to play and weave stories. There's also the added challenge of creating moving parts. Your little engineer will have to impart a bit of trial and error to get the arms and legs to move freely.

Who's It For?

Best for kids ages 5+

Time Commitment

90 minutes to 2 hours

Mess Level

Sawdust and paint

What You Need

⅛-inch plywood

Pencil

Drill

Dremel scroll saw or clamps and fine-tooth saw

Masking tape

120 grit sandpaper

Fine-gauge wire

Wire cutters or scissors

¼-inch drill bit

Wood glue

6 x ¼-inch dowel

Paint, acrylic or tempera

Brushes

Permanent or regular markers

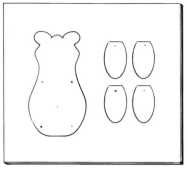

1. Begin by drawing a simple body shape on the wood. Next, draw the arms and legs in 1 or 2 sections each. Mark with a pencil on the body, arms, and legs where you will drill small holes to feed the wire through. Mark where you will drill a hole in the approximate center of the body for the dowel handle. (See illustration.)

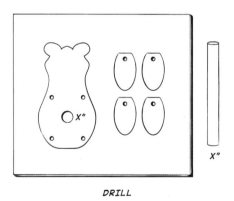

DRILL

2. Drill the marked holes from the front side before you cut out the pieces. This will make it much easier and safer to make all those holes.

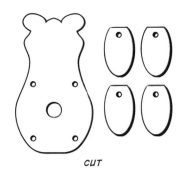

CUT

3. Cut each piece out using the scroll saw. (See illustration.) If you find that the edges splinter when you go to cut or drill, cover the piece of wood with masking tape on the front and back to reduce splintering. It will peel off easily.

4. Sand each segment around the edges and in the hole.

   TIP: Roll a small piece of sandpaper around a toothpick, insert into the drilled holes and sand.

5. Cut a piece of plywood, 3–4 x 12 inches, for the dancing base.

6. Cut four 4-inch segments of fine-gauge wire. Feed the wire through the attachment points; twist the wire together, then bend it over. If the wire ends feel too pokey, use a small piece of tape to cover the twisted ends. The attachment points should be loose and floppy to create movement. (See illustration.) The movement of the pieces against each other and the dancing board will make a sweet clicking sound.

ATTACH (& DECORATE)

7. Color, paint, and decorate to your heart's content.

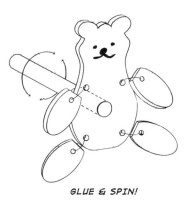

GLUE & SPIN!

8. Add a dab of wood glue and insert the dowel handle into the hole.

HOW TO PLAY

1. Holding the limberjack by the dowel handle, place the legs of the limberjack just above the dancing board, turn on some music, sing a silly song, and twist and move the limberjack to strike the legs on the board making a happy, tappy tune.

➻ What is a folk art tradition?

➻ How do traditions move from place to place?

➻ How do music and craft go together?

Extensions

FOR EVERYONE

➻ Grab your favorite instruments and start a jam band with your limberjack as the dancing star!

FOR KIDS AGES 4 AND UNDER / DELAYED MOTOR SKILLS

➻ Collaborate on the design. This is a great project to help young brains see all of the parts and pieces of a body.

➻ Cut for your kiddo.

FOR KIDS AGES 8 AND UP / ADVANCED MOTOR AND CREATIVE SKILLS

➻ There are more advanced limberjack plans—with wooden joints and more—out there.

➻ Take a trip to the library to research other folk art toy and puppetry traditions.

FOURTEEN

TOY CARS

When my oldest was a baby, my aunt gave him a copy of *Cars and Trucks and Things That Go* by Richard Scarry. It would be an understatement to say that he loved that book. We read each page over and over. It's silly. It's imaginative. A pickle car? A banana mobile? What if real life was that absurd? It'd be great! Milo loved the imaginative ways in which Richard Scarry portrayed his world. I think it also helped that all the characters were animals. Milo would be happiest if all humans were replaced with animal versions of themselves. He would then imagine himself in Busytown. One day he'd be Papa Pig, the next Mistress Mouse. He'd play the part, but it would inevitably change and shift to suit his environment, what props he had on hand, what costume bits I was willing to put together. Communities and all of their moving parts are rich with inspiration for creative play. I especially love all the silliness of unlikely scenes, such as a little mouse driving a piece of cheese.

When I discovered wooden wheels and axles, I was inspired to develop this toy car project. It's a simple provocation—a base and four wheels—and the rest is up to the maker. Using the world of Richard Scarry as inspiration, we've seen kids create everything from complex machines with cranes and dumpers to squirrel cars and whale-mobiles.

What Else Is Possible?

Play is inspired by the input we receive from the world around us, the books we read, the games we play, the shows we watch. It wouldn't work any other way. We have to have input to create output. The creative part of play is how we take all that we know and combine it to create new, novel experiences.

There are many ways to think about play and children. We can see how pretend play prepares children for real-world activities and decision-making. We can see how it helps children develop reason and social skills. What about creative play? Have you ever stopped to notice the way kids develop their imaginative play with one another? One kiddo has an idea. The other child adds on a layer of play, thought, or action—maybe it's just a new sound or movement. They cooperate and cocreate in a fluid way. Sure, there's conflict, sticky points, and frustration. Don't we all feel that way when we're creating something from nothing?

I once heard the simplest and most profound definition of creativity, and it has stuck with me for nearly a decade. Creativity at its core is simply asking yourself, "What

else is possible?" With this simple question our minds are opened to the mere thought that something else really is possible, that what we're looking at, feeling, or touching can somehow be changed, altered, and added to. It's invigorating to just pose the question. From my experience, this reaction isn't just my own. When we pose this question to children as they make and play, they draw upon their own internal resources to ideate, to make that connection just beyond what they already know.

TOY CARS

Let's get rolling! A rolling toy has been a beloved staple of childhood play for centuries. With quality guiding questions, this rolling toy project will get your children thinking about how things work and how to combine unlikely concepts to create fantastic and silly objects. As a bonus—they'll come away with a toy that provides hours of opportunity for play.

Who's It For?

- Best for kids ages 5+

Time Commitment

- 90 minutes to 2 hours

Mess Level

- Sawdust

What You Need

- One 6-inch piece of 1 x 4-inch common board

- Drill with ¼-inch drill bit (or whatever matches the size of your axle)

- Wooden wheels and axles (available at most craft stores or online)

- Hammer

- Scrap wood

- Cool junk, such as bottle caps, popsicle sticks, beads, nuts and bolts

- Hot glue

- Tempera or acrylic paint

- Paintbrushes

- Markers, permanent or regular

OPTIONAL

- Eye hook
- String

TIP: *I can't sing the praises of tempera cakes enough! They last forever, reduce mess, and provide vibrant color on almost all surfaces, with the exception of smooth plastics.*

Tempera sticks are nifty paint sticks that look like glue sticks and are easy to use for little hands. They replace liquid paint and markers, dry quickly, and work on a variety of surfaces.

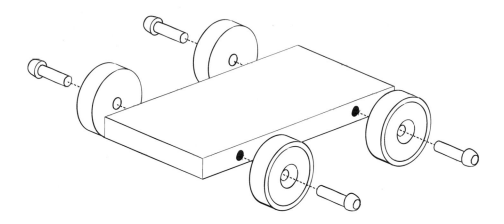

1. Drill holes on the sides of your board for wheels and axles. (See illustration.)

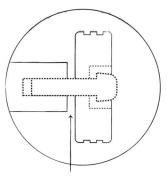

LEAVE ROOM
FOR ROLLING!

2. Assemble wheels and axles according to the manufacturer's directions. Hammer the wheels and axles into the base. (See illustration.)

3. Using scrap wood and all your cool junk, assemble your unique design using a low-temperature hot glue gun. Add details such as headlights, license plates, moving parts, dump-truck features, and so on.

4. After you've attached all your parts and pieces, paint or color your creation.

Tempera paint adheres well to wood but not plastic additions. It's best to use permanent markers on plastics.

5. Optional: Drill a small pilot hole for the eye hook. Twist the eye hook into the hole and attach a string to create a pull toy.

Guiding Questions

➡ What are simple machines?

➡ How do wheels and axles help us do our work and live our lives?

➡ What is the purpose of your toy car?

➡ How will you build it so that it's strong and sturdy enough to play with?

➡ How can you make it silly, innovative, purposeful?

Extensions

FOR EVERYONE

➡ Create a track for your pull toy using masking tape on the carpet.

➡ Create multiple cars that attach together to make a train.

FOR KIDS AGES 4 AND UNDER / DELAYED MOTOR SKILLS

➡ Assist small hands with hammering and attaching items.

FOR KIDS AGES 8 AND UP / ADVANCED MOTOR AND CREATIVE SKILLS

➡ Design and cut a stand-up rolling toy using your scroll saw or bandsaw; attach wheels to the narrow side of the block.

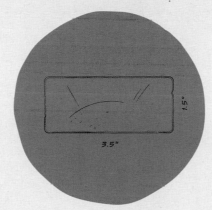

FIFTEEN

2 X 4 CHALLENGE

Material challenges are one of my favorite tinker-style provocations for children of all age ranges. I don't think it was until I was in college, in art school, that I was first introduced to this process. Our assignment was to use duct tape to create a sculpture. That's it. No theme, no additional requirements—just make something with duct tape. One student made an entire outfit, another a self-portrait. I made a cocktail apron. The point is that we all approached the process differently. This is one of the greatest gifts of making with other people—we get to see the ways people generate ideas, make plans, and execute those plans when we all start out in the same room with the same supplies and materials. The only difference—our minds.

clock in the garage, the way my husband rebuilt his bike three times over. It's casual experimentation and, in many ways, it can be historically associated with acceptable forms of play for adults.

Now when it comes to kids, shouldn't it be the same? Tinkering, building, and crafting for the sake of the experience, the time lost in thought to the project at hand? Problems are often solved, but maybe not. Maybe it's all a flop. It's okay for experiences not to be outcome-driven. Let me say that again: it's okay for experiences not to be outcome-driven. We tinker and play because it feels good. If you must have an outcome, doing an activity that feels good typically leads to more good feelings. That's enough for me.

Work for the sake of work is real. Humans have to do things. Given the choice between something, even a chore, we will choose the chore over doing nothing. There's tinkering for the sake of tinkering, for play, to whittle away the hours. There's another function of tinkering beyond the pure joy of taking things apart and seeing how they work. When we tinker, we innovate. We're actively fixing, trying new solutions, moving things around, problem-solving. That's really good for growing brains. Innovation happens. Tinkerers are actively reimagining all around them, from the workbench to the world.

Tinker, Design, Innovate

The tinker movement has been huge in the past five years. When we first opened the shop, it seemed that the only people who knew the term *tinker* were the grandparents who brought their kids to the shop as a nostalgic experience that reminded them of their own time spent tinkering in their garages and shops. At its core, the word *tinker* means "play." Tinkering to me was the way my grandfather messed around with his cuckoo

CREATE YOUR OWN CHALLENGE

Ready to come up with your own challenge? A challenge project is one in which limits are set to drive the work. This could be a limit on materials, such as the 2 x 4 Challenge below, or something else. Below is a list of challenge provocations to get you thinking.

MATERIAL CHALLENGE:

Present one or a limited number of materials with which to create.

FUNCTION CHALLENGE:

Choose a function: this could be as simple as making something that rolls or as complex as a machine that ties your shoes. This is a great way to get kids thinking about design and making things with a purpose.

BE A _____ CHALLENGE:

Using whatever materials and tools you choose, challenge your makers to think like artists or inventors while they're working. For example, how would an artist use these materials?

COLOR CHALLENGE:

Choose a limited color palette and go from there.

ATTACHMENT CHALLENGE:

Create something using only tape, brads, slots, and so forth, for attachments.

TIME CHALLENGE:

Only have five minutes? Have two hours? Challenge your kiddos to create something fresh in a limited time.

With an inexpensive or upcycled 2 x 4, this challenge combines design-thinking strategies with engineering, practical tool use, and creative play. Feel free to add another layer to this project with an additional challenge, such as "Create an object that you can sit on" or "Create an object with moving parts." We've taken this challenge as far as making a tiny house–style playhouse with multiple 2 x 4s. It could be as simple as making a set of blocks by cutting a variety of lengths and angles, then sanding and painting the pieces.

Who's It For?

➡ Best for kids ages 5+

Time Commitment

➡ 90 minutes to many hours

Mess Level

➡ Sawdust

What You Need

➡ One 6- to 8-foot piece 2 x 4 board

➡ Miter saw or handsaw

➡ Wood glue

➡ Drill and various bits

➡ Screws (1 to 2¾ inches in length)

➡ Paper

➡ Pencil

➡ Speed square

➡ Tape measure

➡ 120 grit sand paper

OPTIONAL

➡ Hot glue (wood or regular)

➡ Rope

➡ Paint, any type

THE TRUTH ABOUT "2X4S"

1.5"

3.5"

1. This challenge is all about planning. Spend some time brainstorming all the ways to use a 2 x 4 using the guiding questions below.

2. Now get practical. What can be built in the time you have, with the limited materials you have, with the tools you have, in the space you have?

3. Plans should include dimensions and a cut list. A cut list is simply a rundown of all of the pieces and dimensions you will need to assemble your finished product.

4. Measure twice, cut once. It's important to make accurate cuts so as to reduce waste and create stable construction. Cut all pieces before you begin to assemble your creation.

5. Decide on how you will attach and secure all the parts and pieces of the creation. Screws, hot glue, and even lashing with rope or cordage are all viable options.

Guiding Questions

➤➤ What is the purpose of this object? Is it useful and artistic?

➤➤ What can we create with these materials?

➤➤ Where do my ideas come from?

➤➤ How can we create secure attachments and stable structures using these materials?

➤➤ How do we use a tape measure?

Extensions

FOR EVERYONE

➤➤ Provide more materials! More wood, upcycled junk, paint, and so forth.

➤➤ Do this challenge on a mini scale. Use furring strips or even popsicle sticks. I've even seen 1:12 scale mini lumber available online.

FOR KIDS AGES 4 AND UNDER / DELAYED MOTOR SKILLS

➤➤ Collaborate, collaborate, collaborate.

FOR KIDS AGES 8 AND UP / ADVANCED MOTOR AND CREATIVE SKILLS

➤➤ Allow older kids to operate power tools with close supervision.

➤➤ Create a more specific challenge, such as making a bench, play structure, or teeter-totter.

PART FOUR

TINKER, BUILD, AND PLAY

I was teaching a printmaking workshop at a local library the other day. The library had the most remarkable maker space. It was filled to the brim with cool tech. A 3D printer? Check. A laser cutter? Check. In all honesty, I felt out of my element. I am a low-tech human, through and through. Many kids have access to some pretty cool tech resources in libraries and schools, and many organizations and families in the STEAM movement place a high value on teaching kids to be tech savvy, and for good reason. Knowing how to use current technology is important for fully participating in the world around us. However, when we're thinking about outcomes for our children, we can set them up for success by simply allowing them to play and create using everyday objects.

Our most popular curriculum at C&A is a course entitled Toy Shop. In this program, kids learn to make their own playthings, such as a stuffie or a rolling toy. They also design and create their own line of toys and then "buy and sell" their items to one another using pretend money. There's something inherently satisfying about making your own playthings, and that's what this chapter is all about. Playing while making and making to play. From junk robots to a tiny town, these projects are built to be fun to make and fun to play with, too.

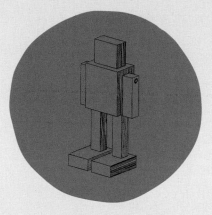

SIXTEEN

JUNK
ROBOTS

The other day at the shop, we were making kitty cat–inspired work and one kiddo decided to only speak in meows. I went along and pretty soon all ten kids were communicating only in meows. I saw a few parents roll their eyes at the silliness of four-year-olds meowing at one another and at me, but isn't that the beauty of kids? They're all silly!

This project is all about embracing silliness, and it's by far the most popular project we host at the shop. Junk robots are the perfect platform for silliness. Robots help us do jobs that people might not want to do. I always begin this project by asking kids to close their eyes and imagine a robot that does a job that helps people do things they don't want to do. I then ask them to imagine a robot that does two jobs that are very

different. A robot that does homework and washes the car? Yes, please! A robot that sweeps the floor and makes my coffee—even better!

Silly things are silly because they're unexpected. Silly things combine dissimilar things in peculiar ways. Remember Richard Scarry's pickle car? Making silly things leads to innovation. When we combine unlikely pairs, new ideas emerge. We often think of very young children as those who benefit the most from play and playful behaviors, but I would suggest that all people, regardless of age, could benefit from more playful and silly behavior. Nothing like making robot and cat sounds to pull us out of a sour mood. Silliness doesn't need to lead to wild or uncontrolled behavior; rather, it's a product of imaginative play. Kids are naturally funny. Let's harness the funny to be more creative and more playful in our making practices.

Making Time to Play

Kids ask about a million questions a day (okay, more like four hundred). As caregivers, all of those requests piled on top of our everyday adult jobs can feel, well, frustrating. How can we slow down and make time to play, to answer all of those questions? Sometimes we have to force ourselves to dedicate the time to really listen to our kids. Creative playtime can be a time for us to hear our kids (even their bad jokes). Try building dedicated work-play into your time with your kids. This can look and feel all sorts of ways. One strategy that I've used with my students and my own children is to make alongside them. I will start working on my own version of the same project they're on. I will work alongside a child, narrate my own process, joke around about my failures, and chat about everyday stuff. Here are a few playful conversation starters:

➤ Would you rather _____ or _____ ? (This is my youngest son's all-time favorite question. Just keep it clean!)

➤ Tell me your best joke.

➤ What's the weirdest thing that's ever happened to you?

➤ Tell me about a time you had a big belly laugh.

Who's It For?

➤ Best for kids ages 4+

Time Commitment

➤ 90 minutes to 2 hours

Mess Level

➤ Sawdust and glue

What You Need

Scrap wood

Hammer and nails

Hot glue

Screws

Nuts and bolts

Wire

Bottle caps (plastic and metal)

Drill with a variety of bits

Paint, tempera or acrylic

Paintbrushes

Markers

OPTIONAL

Tin cans

Nails

Corks (make great jet packs!)

Clothespins

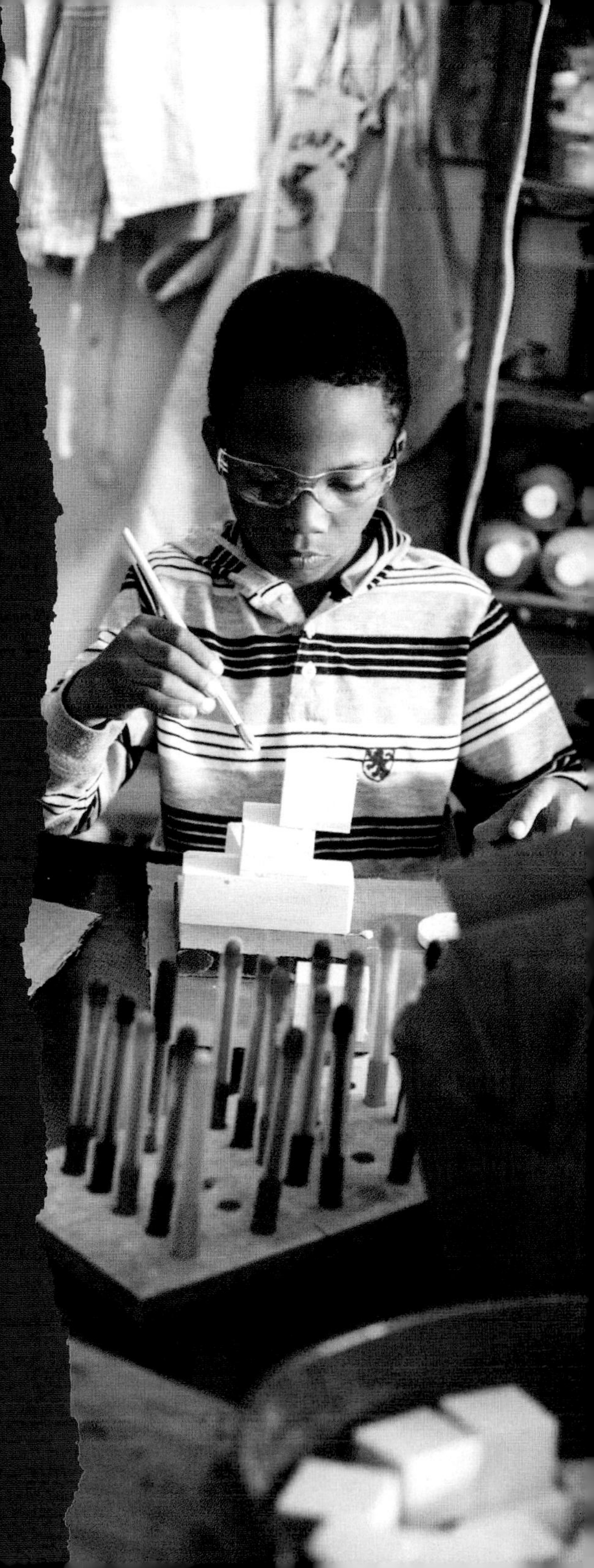

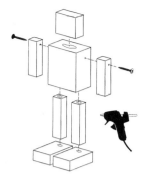

1. Determine the body of your robot. This could be a tin can, a block of wood, or whatever cool scrap of junk you have around.

2. Gather materials suitable for legs, arms, head, and so forth.

3. Lay out all of your parts and pieces and play with different ways of assembling your parts. There's no wrong way to make a robo-friend!

4. If you'd like to add moving parts, drill small pilot holes in the arms and/or legs of your robot and screw them into the body.

5. Using glue, assemble the remaining body parts of your robot.

6. Add embellishments such as bolts for eyes or wire for antennae; bottle caps attached with nails make great twisting buttons. Go for the details here. Each attachment should have a job to do (real or imagined).

7. Just as with the rolling toy, paint after adding all of your embellishments. Permanent markers can be used on any plastic parts.

8. Don't forget to play! Junk robots often become play buddies that enable hours of imaginative play.

Guiding Questions
➼ What's the robot's job?

➼ What's a job you have that you'd love for the robot to do?

➼ How can we create moving parts?

➼ Why do details matter?

Extensions
FOR EVERYONE
➼ Make it big or small. Playing with scale is a great way to drive creative play.

➼ Create a block city for your robot to explore.

➼ Add dollar-store LED lights.

FOR KIDS AGES 4 AND UNDER / DELAYED MOTOR SKILLS
➼ Use Velcro tabs to attach and reattach parts.

FOR KIDS AGES 8 AND UP / ADVANCED MOTOR AND CREATIVE SKILLS
➼ Use power tools to cut, attach, and create parts.

SEVENTEEN

TINY TOWN

There's a specialness to miniatures that is universal to children. For
the past year, I've been teaching an afterschool club called Tiny Town.
In that time, my small group of kiddos has made everything under the
sun in miniature. We've explored materials, themes, and construction
techniques—from polymer clay and shrink film to papier-mâché and
wire. Making things on a small scale allows children to be in control of
an environment, examine the details of their external world, and engage
in imaginative play independently.

I grew up in the suburbs of Chicago, and my favorite outing
was a day spent in the Thorne Miniature Rooms in the basement

of the Art Institute of Chicago. The dark basement was illuminated by windows filled with precise miniatures of period-era spaces. Each window depicted a room that was meticulously recreated in miniature. I was always enchanted by the level of precision and detail of the spaces. It was pure magic. I would press my nose against the glass and imagine myself in an eighteenth-century drawing room. Then, when I was eight years old, my brother and mom gifted me a huge Victorian-style dollhouse, which took them months to paint, decorate, and finish. My big brother even made the chimney look like real brick. It was one of the most thoughtful gifts I've ever received. I would play house for hours, placing and rearranging the furniture and family that lived inside. I would use all my craft supplies to make tiny additions to the house, like dishes and wire glasses for the little boy who lived inside. (I've worn glasses since I can remember.)

Practicing for Life

Making miniature worlds can be as much about the play that happens after as the making itself. Don't forget to allow time for children to engage with the objects they create. This is an important extension of the process of making and one of the most profound aspects of making useful objects with children. With miniatures in particular, children are able to imagine themselves in the worlds they've created. They develop stories, and perhaps even more profoundly, they will often work out interpersonal scenarios happening in their real lives. They've chosen the players and the scenes while in the creation phase and they often represent their current emotional state in some way. Play therapy is a thing for a reason. Little brains don't always know how to articulate big feelings. By making creative play a safe space, we give children the opportunity to express the inner workings of their hearts and minds.

Making beautiful, process-oriented art is fantastic and an integral part of the creative lives of children. However, I experienced a profound shift in my own ideology in that children benefit so much from making objects that they can then use, manipulate, and integrate into their lives. Don't forget to jump in and play with your children's handmade things. They'll be so proud that you've taken an interest in learning about and engaging in their completed work. You may also learn more about what's really going on in those little brains of theirs.

Just like junk robots, this project is all about using the materials you have on hand in innovative ways. There's no wrong way to make things in miniature. It's really all about creating an imaginative environment. Creating a tiny world allows your makers to explore endless possibilities. It could be a realistic representation, such as a mountain scene, or a fantastic unicorn habitat. The options are endless.

Who's It For?

➡ Best for kids ages 4+

Time Commitment

➡ 90 minutes to many days on end

Mess Level

➡ Hot glue and small bits

What You Need

This is a fairly open-ended provocation. Use what you have on hand. Below is a list of items we frequently use for this project.

➡ Cardboard or plywood base with a back, or a shoebox

➡ Cool junk such as pompoms, corks, caps, sticks, fabric bits, etc.

➡ Hot glue

➡ Peg dolls

➡ Wire

➡ Colored paper

➡ Paint, tempera or acrylic

➡ Paintbrushes

➡ Markers, permanent or regular

➡ Cardstock

➡ Wire

➡ Polymer clay

➡ Air-dry clay

➡ Shrink film

➡ Tinfoil

TIP: *Tweezers are a great for placing small items where hot glue will be applied. Also it's just plain fun and great hand-eye-coordination practice to pick up tiny things with tweezers.*

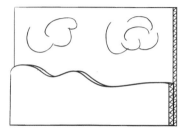

BACKGROUND

ROLLING HILLS, FARAWAY VISTAS, CLOUDS

1. Starting with a base, use the guiding questions to determine what your miniature world will look like. Begin with the background. Add all of the details that are farthest away. This can be accomplished by painting, drawing, or collage. (See illustration). If it's an outdoor scene, discuss how objects seem smaller when they're far away. I like to have kids close one eye and attempt to pinch faraway objects between their fingers.

SCENERY

SCENERY, WATERFALLS, RIVERS, TREES

2. Move on to the objects that are in the middle ground. These are the pieces that are still a bit far but not at the back. These items may also be the permanent pieces of the work. This is where you can get creative with materials and construction techniques. (See illustration.)

FOREGROUND

MINIATURES! FIRE, ANIMALS, CAMPSITE

3. Lastly, create the objects closest in the scene and the movable details. These can include furniture, books, food, people, animals, and more. (See illustration.)

TIP: I like to start with a brief discussion of scale and proportion. Scale is how big or small something is compared to our bodies. Proportion is how big or small something is compared to other objects. For instance, the artist Claes Oldenburg is famous for recreating everyday objects on a massive scale—for example, a cherry as big as me! Proportion can be explained by examining a table and chairs. The table must be suited in size to the chair, otherwise the proportions are off. If the chair is too large, no one would be able to sit in the chair and slide up to the table; the chair is out of proportion. Scale for a dollhouse is typically shrunk to 1:12, meaning that for every 1 foot (12 inches) in real life, the object is recreated at 1 inch. This can be tricky for kids to comprehend, but an approximation is fine.

Guiding Questions

➤ Imagine a place inside or outside, real or pretend—what does it look like?

➤ Why did you choose this scene?

➤ What are the farthest details you can see?

➤ What is in the middle?

➤ What is closest to you?

➤ How can you use scale and proportion to create a believable scene?

Extensions

FOR EVERYONE

➤ Create multiple rooms.

➤ Research different ecosystems, architectural styles, and so forth.

➤ Play, play, play.

FOR KIDS AGES 4 AND UNDER / DELAYED MOTOR SKILLS

➤ Tiny things can be hard for little hands. Try upping the scale and using a large box for little ones to create a world of their own. Cutting, pasting, and painting can be a great first step.

FOR KIDS AGES 8 AND UP / ADVANCED MOTOR AND CREATIVE SKILLS

➤ Use $1/8$-inch plywood to construct a more elaborate structure.

➤ Weave mini rugs to add to your space.

➤ Create your own wallpaper with unique patterns and designs.

➤ Many hobby stores sell copper tape to illuminate your miniatures.

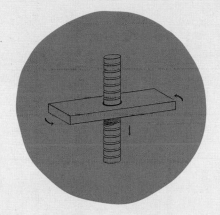

EIGHTEEN

SIMPLE MACHINES

This challenge project tasks kids to approach simple machines from the attitude of an artist, an inventor, or a builder. Each vocational approach demands a different way of thinking and problem-posing. If an artist uses simple machines to create a moving work of art, the set of challenges is quite different than a builder constructing a crane or ramp. As an inventor, a child must find a common problem to solve using the basic technology of simple machines. Simple machines are tools; how we use them is wholly dependent on our needs and desired outcomes.

When we task a child to think like a builder or an artist, we can direct them to more fully consider their approach to the making process. The STEAM movement has placed a lot of emphasis on the engineering aspect of problem-solving. I prefer to take a more wholistic approach to the maker movement. Creative problem-solving is a skill that all people need. In the simple machines challenge, you will see

a variety of challenges that enable makers to work from a point of view that suits them best while developing an understanding of the mechanics and endless uses of simple machines in our daily lives.

STEAM sans Electricity

Here in Colorado, most second graders learn all about simple machines. A few years back, I worked with a local school to develop a hands-on culminating project for a group of highly gifted kiddos. When I started diving into the curriculum, I discovered that simple machines are the backbone of human innovation. How cool is that? We use simple machines every day often without stopping to admire how much these simple inventions do for us. Often in the STEAM movement, the focus is on current technology, on computer-based tech. I am a firm believer that for kids to truly understand current technologies, we must teach them from the beginning. This is one of the reasons that I love heritage skills and why I believe that nontech tinkering is so valuable for kids. Simple machines enable us to make the most our lives. From cars and bikes, to cranes and elevators, the world is powered by simple machines that enable the more advanced technology so many of us rely on.

SIMPLE MACHINES

This project is a great opportunity to have kids explore innovation from the point of view of an inventor, artist, or engineer. Below are a few simple machine–specific challenge prompts to choose from. As with all of the projects in this section, use what you have! The best part of tinkering is finding new uses for discarded objects. Below I list some of my favorite simple-machine objects and tools.

Who's It For?

➤ Best for kids ages 4+

Time Commitment

➤ 1 to 2 hours

Mess Level

➤ Glue and paint

What You Need

As with all of these creative challenges, use what you have on hand. Below is a list of suggested materials.

➤ Low-temp hot glue

➤ Scrap wood

➤ Brads

➤ Popsicle sticks

➤ String

➤ Bolts

➤ Washers

➤ Cardboard tubes

➤ Cardboard

➤ Bottle caps and nails (as wheels and axles)

➤ Beads

➤ Tempera or acrylic paint

➤ Paintbrushes

➤ Markers, permanent or regular

1. Use 1 or more simple machines to complete the challenges below. When 2 simple machines are combined, it's known as a compound machine. Here are 6 basic machines:

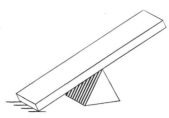

LEVER

A tool that pries something. A lever moves against a fulcrum, or the point on which the lever pivots. Think an ice cream scoop or the end of a hammer.

WHEEL AND AXLE

A round object turns around an axle or cylindrical post, causing movement.

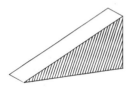

INCLINE PLANE

Think ramps.

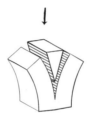

WEDGE

The pointed edge of an inclined plane that can be used to pry things apart. An ax blade is a wedge.

PULLEY

A modification of the wheel in which a cord wraps around the wheel. As the cord moves around the wheel, it's able to pull an object attached to the cord. This allows the user to raise, lower, and move objects with less force.

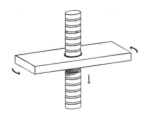

SCREW

Imagine that an inclined plane is wrapped around a cylinder. The screw turns and is able to move through a solid surface with ease.

2. The challenges:

INVENTOR CHALLENGE:

Invent a compound machine that helps do a job in your home. Scissors are a great example of a compound machine (wedge and lever); the same goes for a knife (wedge and lever).

INVENTOR CHALLENGE:

Create a simple-machine toy using only four objects. Just as in the 2 x 4 Challenge (page 119), limiting material choices can lead to innovation.

INVENTOR CHALLENGE:

Artist Challenge: Create a work of art with movement. The kinetic work of the artist Alexander Calder is a fantastic inspiration, especially the videos of his Cirque Calder. He used simple materials such as fabric and wire to create an interactive experience that is quite lovely in its simplicity and playfulness.

INVENTOR CHALLENGE:

Builder Challenge: Design and create a structure that moves people from low to high.

Guiding Questions

➤ What are simple machines?

➤ How do they help us in our everyday lives?

➤ How do people use simple machines?

➤ How can we use simple and compound machines to invent and innovate?

Extensions

FOR EVERYONE

➤ Go big! There are amazing examples of Rube Goldberg machines all over the internet. Rube Goldberg was a cartoonist and artist who became well known for his cartoon depictions of overly complicated contraptions completing simple tasks. A Rube Goldberg machine is a complex-machine-system that does a simple job, such as pouring a bowl of cereal. This is a great rainy-day activity.

FOR KIDS AGES 4 AND UNDER / DELAYED MOTOR SKILLS

➤ I always introduce simple machines with ramps. Little ones love to build car and marble runs using simple materials such as cardboard tubes, blocks, flat cardboard, and masking tape. They can set things up and position ramps with a little trial and error.

FOR KIDS AGES 8 AND UP / ADVANCED MOTOR AND CREATIVE SKILLS

➤ Talk to your maker about prototyping. A prototype is an experiment in physical form. When we create and invent, we prototype. Most likely our first attempt at something new isn't going to be our best possible version. A challenge project can be created in iterations—in other words, create your object based on the challenge, then reflect, ask for feedback, and refine. Refinement may look like creating a second draft, adding, taking away, repairing, reengineering, adding color, and so forth.

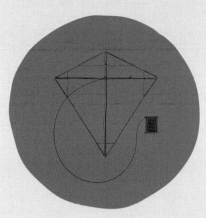

NINETEEN

MINI KITES

Kites are the perfect example of a simple childhood pleasure that, once revealed, is imbued with so much science and complex systems. This is the beauty of childhood play in a nutshell. Children intuitively learn complex aspects of life and the way the world works through play. Children are built to play—and what is play but a rehearsal for life? Children pretend within social roles and jobs; they imagine the spaces beyond their reach. They invent, create, refine, and define themselves through play. To the external eye, they might just be lying in a field with a kite on a string.

A Brief History of How Kids Make and Play

Throughout history and culture, the ways in which children play has been determined by the social trends occurring at the time. For instance, we currently live in a culture that often values structured play, sports, music lessons, and super-specified toys over free play. When our children are playing, it's often solitary, adult-supervised, or facilitated play. Think of the single child playing with blocks or going on a bike ride with Dad. While I had all of these structured play options in my childhood, between the ages six and eleven I spent the majority of my time outside, supervised only by my big brother and the neighborhood kids. We played in the forest. We built forts. We played made-up games. We explored. What seems to have shifted dramatically in the past thirty years is what we believe children to be capable of.

I have a bit of an obsession with vintage and antique craft and how-to manuals for children. What's revealed in these books is the attitudes toward children at the time they were written. I have many from the early twentieth century that deem boys to be almost completely wild and best left to the outdoors until age sixteen or seventeen. Books for girls from this same era portray girls as homebound but capable of refined and complex levels of handwork, all in an era when many children were working on farms and in factories.

In the 1950s, guided by *Popular Mechanics* and home economics books, children and young adults were building a better and brighter country through handcrafted items and resourcefulness at home.

Along came the 1970s and my favorite book of all time comes out: *Housebuilding for Children* by Lester Walker. In *Housebuilding for Children*, Walker focuses on the resourcefulness of children. Written for the child reader age eight to ten, his book demonstrates the trust he had in the ability of children to build big things safely and collaboratively. The child is precocious and strong, playful and mistake-prone, but also totally capable of building a house out of old mattresses found in a junkyard!

Our adult expectations for how children should play is informed by our own childhood experiences, what we believe about child development, the media, and culture. What we believe about childhood play is a direct reflection of our societal norms. In a simple sense, we get what we expect. Of course, some parts of a child's developing brain can be set to a timeline that is fairly predictable. But as I've said before, when we become careful observers of our children and ourselves, we're better able to truly see what our children are capable of and what we're doing to either facilitate their play or, conversely, what we may be doing to stifle and limit our children.

As caregivers and facilitators of childhood, it's important for us to take a step back and examine why we believe what we believe about play and creativity. Why we encourage certain activities and behaviors and diminish others. After a lifetime of work with elementary school–age children and being the mother of two, I believe that creative and builder tasks are best approached from an attitude of trust; that if we offer children opportunities to create—and that may even just be by offering them time to be bored, to create in their own minds—they will choose to do so.

THE BENEFITS OF BOREDOM

So far, we've explored all sorts of directed work and play. However, I want to take a moment to emphasize the value of boredom. Yes, boredom! We've all heard a child lament about how bored they are. My mom would say, "That's too bad. What are you going to do about it?" I'll say it here—you're not responsible for your child's entertainment. You're responsible for providing a safe and loving environment for children to be themselves. You're responsible for helping them learn how to seek knowledge, pleasure, and challenges in healthy ways. Ask yourself if your parents jumped to attention when you expressed boredom. Mine certainly didn't. But what my mom would also say is, "Would you like some suggestions?"

Recently my children were complaining about their own boredom for what felt like the hundredth Saturday in a row. I said, "Okay, let's brainstorm some ideas." The rules: the activities couldn't involve screens, adult assistance, spending money, or getting in a car. We wrote each idea out on a strip of cardstock and placed them in a jar on the counter. Suggestions for two fairly independent kids ages eight and eleven included:

MAKE SOMETHING

- Write a story
- Read a book
- Walk to the library
- Play football
- Skateboard
- Ride bikes
- Play with building blocks
- Play with the dog
- Draw
- Go to the playground

WHAT WOULD YOUR KIDS SUGGEST?

This book is all about helping create a container for work to happen naturally.

And yes, project-specific work is valuable, and parent engagement and collaboration in work-play is important, but we shouldn't shy away from our children's boredom. Boredom means that they're on the edge of action. Boredom is an internal call to motivate, to seek out activity. As caregivers, we can encourage boredom by building unstructured time into our kids' busy lives. Open studio time and unstructured outdoor playtime enables kids to manifest their own entertainment. We as caregivers can set the stage and create both safe and inspiring places for children to thrive. I encourage you to let go. Let your kids get bored. They will become architects of their own play and creative processes.

The first record of kites dates back twenty-five hundred years to China. Kites have been used for military, ceremony, children's play, art, and more. In the 1800s, kites were very popular in the United States among adults and children alike. The Eddy-style kite, a popular and simple diamond-shaped kite with no tail, originated during this time.

Who's It For?

Best for kids ages 5+

Time Commitment

90 minutes to 2 hours

Mess Level

Maybe a little glue

What You Need

Tissue paper, mylar, a plastic bag, or any lightweight material that can be cut easily

Scissors

Ruler or straightedge

Broom corn (synthetic or real; just nip two 6-inch lengths from your kitchen broom) for the spar and the spine

White glue

Sewing machine thread

Clear tape

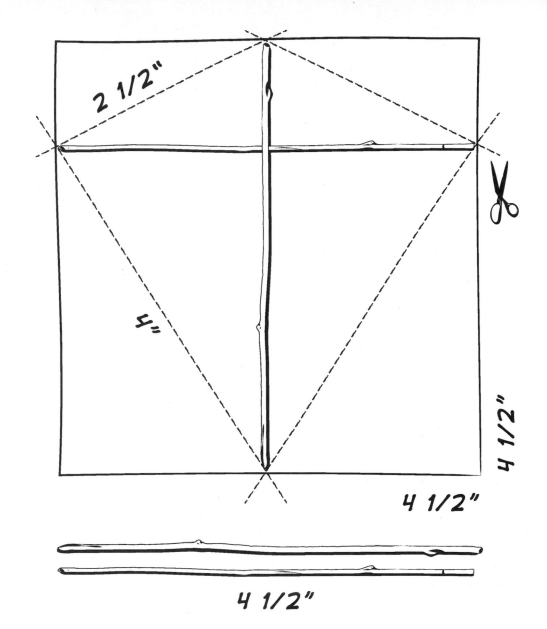

2 1/2"

4"

4 1/2"

4 1/2"

4 1/2"

1. Place your material over the kite pattern above and trace the outline. If the material you're using is opaque, trace the pattern from the book onto a piece of paper, then cut to create a reusable pattern. Cut the kite shape from your kite material.

TINKER, BUILD, AND PLAY

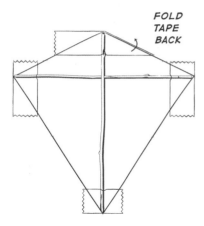

FOLD
TAPE
BACK

to adhere. Add a piece of tape to each attachment point and trim.

5. Tie the sewing thread to the center point of the spare and spine. This is called the tow point or the bridle.

6. Now it's time to fly! Provided your kite is light enough for its size, you should be able to fly it with relative ease.

HOW TO PLAY

1. Here's how to solo launch your mini kite: Head outside on a windy day. How do you know it's the right kind of wind? Here's a helpful aid: Are the leaves rustling, the trees swaying, or the dust blowing? Perfect! Go fly a kite.

2. Stand with your back to the wind.

3. Hold the kite out to your side so that your body isn't creating a wind shadow.

4. Hold the kite up and begin to let out the line between your hands. The kite should catch and begin to rise.

2. Lay the broom corn, one piece on top of the other—one horizonal, the other vertical—on top of the kite cutout to form the spar (the horizontal piece) and the spine (the vertical piece). Trim to the edges of the kite and tape in place.

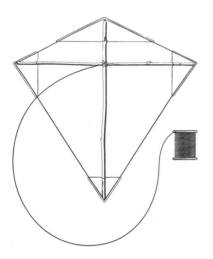

3. Glue and tie together the spar and spine until secure.

4. Place a dab of glue on the end of each side of the spar and spine and lay the pieces back down onto the kite and press

Guiding Questions

➼ How does a kite fly?

➼ What are the aerodynamic forces (gravity and lift)?

➼ How do you think people developed kites? Where might they have found inspiration in nature?

➼ How did kite making help aviation?

➼ How does the design, shape, and size of the kite affect the way it flies?

Extensions

FOR EVERYONE

➼ There are as many kite designs as you can think of! Innovate and test out your own ideas.

FOR KIDS AGES 4 AND UNDER / DELAYED MOTOR SKILLS

➼ Collaborate to make a larger Eddy-style kite. Have little hands be in charge of decorating and painting.

FOR KIDS AGES 8 AND UP / ADVANCED MOTOR AND CREATIVE SKILLS

➼ Research more complex kite construction techniques and attempt to replicate one.

➼ Use a variety of materials. Many kites are now made using ripstop nylon and are machine sewn together.

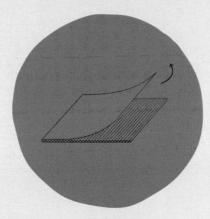

TWENTY

CARDBOARD CREATORS

I've saved the best for last! Cardboard is my all-time favorite and hands down the ultimate maker material. Why? It's free. It's easy to work with. Make it big or small. Mess it up? No big deal; there's another delivery outside. The cardboard box was even inducted into the National Museum of Play in 2005. I'm sure we've all heard at least one story where the child received an expensive toy or gift and all they wanted was to play with the box that it came in. As a former childhood box-dweller myself, I love some good cardboard.

At the shop, we get super excited when we score some good, clean, big, sturdy cardboard. Once we have a crazy amount of cardboard, it's time for some creative play! But it matters how we present it to kids. As facilitators, we have the opportunity to shape the outcome of our kids' play by setting the stage, even for something as open as cardboard play.

Simplify and Limit

I understand that the concepts of simplify and limit can sound almost icky to some. I hear parents say that they don't want to limit their children, that they want them to have choices, and I understand the sentiment. However, when given too many choices, it's in our nature to freeze up. Think of it this way—when you encounter a restaurant menu that's five pages long, that has everything from Caesar salad to sushi, it's hard to choose from so many options. This is true for a child's whole world as well. We can have it all, just not right now.

Simplify. Simplify. Simplify. When we're working with a provocation, the simplification comes with limiting. Let's face it—limits are all around us. Walls, fences, seat belts, and

so on. Limits help us to be safe, to create goals, to become resourceful, to explore and experiment within a safe container. As children get older, the limits, the fences, are moved further out. The container is larger and filled with more complexity. Limiting and simplifying look a lot of different ways. Our 2 x 4 challenges were limited by materials, our miniatures by size, our weavings by the materials we have on hand. When we create our work space and create rules and routines, we're setting limits and simplifying the possible behaviors and interactions. By removing distractions or the limits of too many choices, we allow children to explore and create in a container that, while still rich, is within their reach.

WHAT ARE THE LIMITS OF YOUR CREATIVE PLAY?

Here's a handy checklist that can help drive your thinking when it comes to developing creative build-play with simple and effective limits.

MATERIALS

- What supplies are available?
- How much of each supply is available?

TOOLS

- What tools are/will be made available?

PRODUCT

- What is the project outcome?
- Is it a product, play, or challenge?

TIME

- How much time do you have to complete the task?

SUPPORT

- How much support will you or friends provide?
- Is it an independent task? Is it a collaboration?

SPACE

- Will the product need to be stored or transported?
- How much cleanup time do you have?
- How messy can you/should you be?
- How much noise can you make?

SAFETY/INSTRUCTION

- What do you need to know in order to work safely and successfully?

CARDBOARD CREATORS

Cardboard is one of the easiest and most readily available craft materials out there. (Who doesn't have a pile from all those deliveries?) We use cardboard to create play spaces such as collapsible houses, play stores, sculptures, costumes, marble runs, and more. When working with cardboard, the sky's the limit. See what you have available in terms of space, time, and materials, and go from there. Below are some tips and tricks to guide some serious cardboard creation.

Who's It For?

Best for kids ages 3+

Time Commitment

1 hour to days on end

Mess Level

Cardboard bits

What You Need

Cardboard

Scissors

Hot glue

Elmer's Glue-All multipurpose glue

Masking tape

Clothespins

Tempera paint

Paintbrushes

Markers

1. Define the limits of your cardboard creativity using the checklist on page 155 to develop your own cardboard provocation. Cardboard alone is often enough of an idea starter.

2. Prepare the cardboard as much or as little as you like. We often have a bin with multiple sizes and types of cardboard as a simple provocation.

3. Choose how things will be attached or assembled, using hot glue, liquid glue, masking tape, fasteners, or slots. There are a lot of options to choose from. Here are some ways to attach your cardboard:

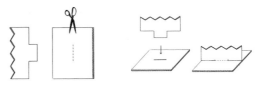

SLOT

Cut a slot in two pieces and slide them together. This strategy creates a T-shaped construction. Slot building is perfect for little hands. Try making a collection of large cardboard shapes with slots. These can be assembled and reassembled time and time again.

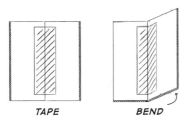

TAPE   BEND

L-BRACE

Use masking tape or strip a layer of cardboard and paste it on to help brace corners or create a hinge.

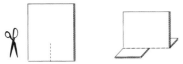

CUT   FOLD & ATTACH

TABS

Similar to a flange, fold back a tab and attach. Tabs can also be used with buttonhole-style slots.

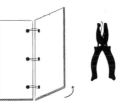

HOLE PUNCH & WIRE

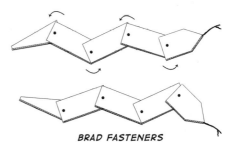

BRAD FASTENERS

HOLE CONSTRUCTION

Use a hole punch to create attachment points. Stitch together with string or wire, or use brads to create moving parts.

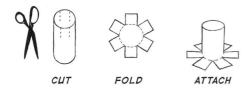

CUT   FOLD   ATTACH

FLANGE

A flange can be created to attach a tube or other structure perpendicular to its base. Cut ½-inch slots around the tube or along the base, then fold these slots to form tabs that can be attached to the base using glue or tape.

PEEL   BEND!   BEND!

CURVES

Strip one side of the paper layer of cardboard to reveal the corrugated inside. This will create a more flexible material perfect for curves.

TIP: Use clothespins to temporarily hold attachments in place when hot gluing.

Guiding Questions

➤➤ Why is cardboard a good building material?

➤➤ How can I cut, bend, and manipulate this material to create an object?

Extensions

FOR EVERYONE

➤➤ Choose one more material to add to your creation. Reflect on how that changes your work.

FOR KIDS AGES 4 AND UNDER / DELAYED MOTOR SKILLS

➤➤ Have even more pieces precut for little hands.

➤➤ Use electrical tape instead of masking tape. It's easier to manipulate.

FOR KIDS AGES 8 AND UP / ADVANCED MOTOR AND CREATIVE SKILLS

➤➤ Pull out that Dremel scroll saw to create epic custom cardboard work. Layer cardboard pieces together, then carve to create sculptures and more.

ACKNOWLEDGMENTS

A huge heartfelt thank you to the following people:

Jonathan—my husband, my big-idea partner. Thank you for believing in me.

Bethany O'Halloran—my mom, my best friend, and my first reader. Thank you for a truly creative childhood and being my person, always.

Ross Holton, my dad, for always being my cheerleader.

Milo and Wyatt, my boys. I'm not sure what life was like before you. Thank you for being my guys and my greatest inspiration.

Daniel Holton, my brother. Thank you for lugging my harp around, installing all those art shows, and for always showing up for me.

Grammy and Grandpa, you showed us what it means to love children with whole hearts.

Aunt Annie, for teaching me about hard work, dedication, and positivity.

Tony Deland—you're the third wheel on our tricycle of life.

Jennifer Brown, for your insight, encouragement, and direction.

Breanna Locke, for your positivity, eye, and insight.

Daniel Evan Quay, for being able to see my vision when I can't even see it myself.

Raine Chism, for your eye.

Anna Loring, thank you for holding down the shop and bringing all of your creative, kid-loving magic to it.

The whole C&A staff—you're the glue of our community.

To my lady crew—Sarah, Zarah, Nichole, Alyssa, Heather, Claire, Jessica, Julia, and Kirsten. You're inspirations to me daily.

ABOUT THE AUTHOR

Delanie Holton-Fessler is a teacher, maker, mom, and founder of The Craftsman & Apprentice, a heritage craft-inspired workshop in Denver, Colorado. She grew up playing in the woods and making messes, art, her own clothes—you name it. Delanie became an elementary school art teacher in 2004, and for ten years she worked in high-poverty schools. In that time, she also worked as a project-based learning specialist and professional artist. Delanie fell for combining real-world and creative work with kids. Making with upward of 750 kids each week for years gave Delanie the working philosophy and foundation for The Craftsman & Apprentice. She opened her shop in 2014 with the simple mission to give people of all ages a space to make and connect to one another. Delanie has since worked with schools, individuals, and organizations to build creative space solutions, and she's lectured on work space aesthetics, creative play, and more. Each day she has the opportunity to gather people together to create and play.